USER CHARGES IN THE SOCIAL SERVICES:
AN ECONOMIC THEORY OF NEED AND INABILITY

Ministry of Education, Ontario
Information Centre, 13th Floor,
Mowat Block, Queen's Park,
Toronto, Ont.   M7A 1L2

MICHAEL KRASHINSKY

User Charges in the Social Services: an economic theory of need and inability

PUBLISHED FOR THE ONTARIO ECONOMIC COUNCIL BY
UNIVERSITY OF TORONTO PRESS
TORONTO BUFFALO LONDON

© Ontario Economic Council 1981
Printed in Canada

Canadian Cataloguing in Publication Data

Krashinsky, Michael, 1947-
User charges in the social services
(Ontario Economic Council research studies, ISSN 0708-3688 ; 24)
Bibliography: p.
ISBN 0-8020-3381-4
1. Welfare economics. 2. Externalities (Economics).
3. Public goods. 4. Public welfare – Ontario.
I. Ontario Economic Council. II. Title. III. Series.
HB99.3.K72   330.15'5   C81-094633-5

This report reflects the views of the author and not necessarily those of the Ontario Economic Council or the Ontario government. The Council establishes policy questions to be investigated and commissions research projects, but it does not influence the conclusions or recommendations of authors. The decision to sponsor publication of this study was based on its competence and relevance to public policy and was made with the advice of anonymous referees expert in the area.

In memory of my father, Harry Krashinsky

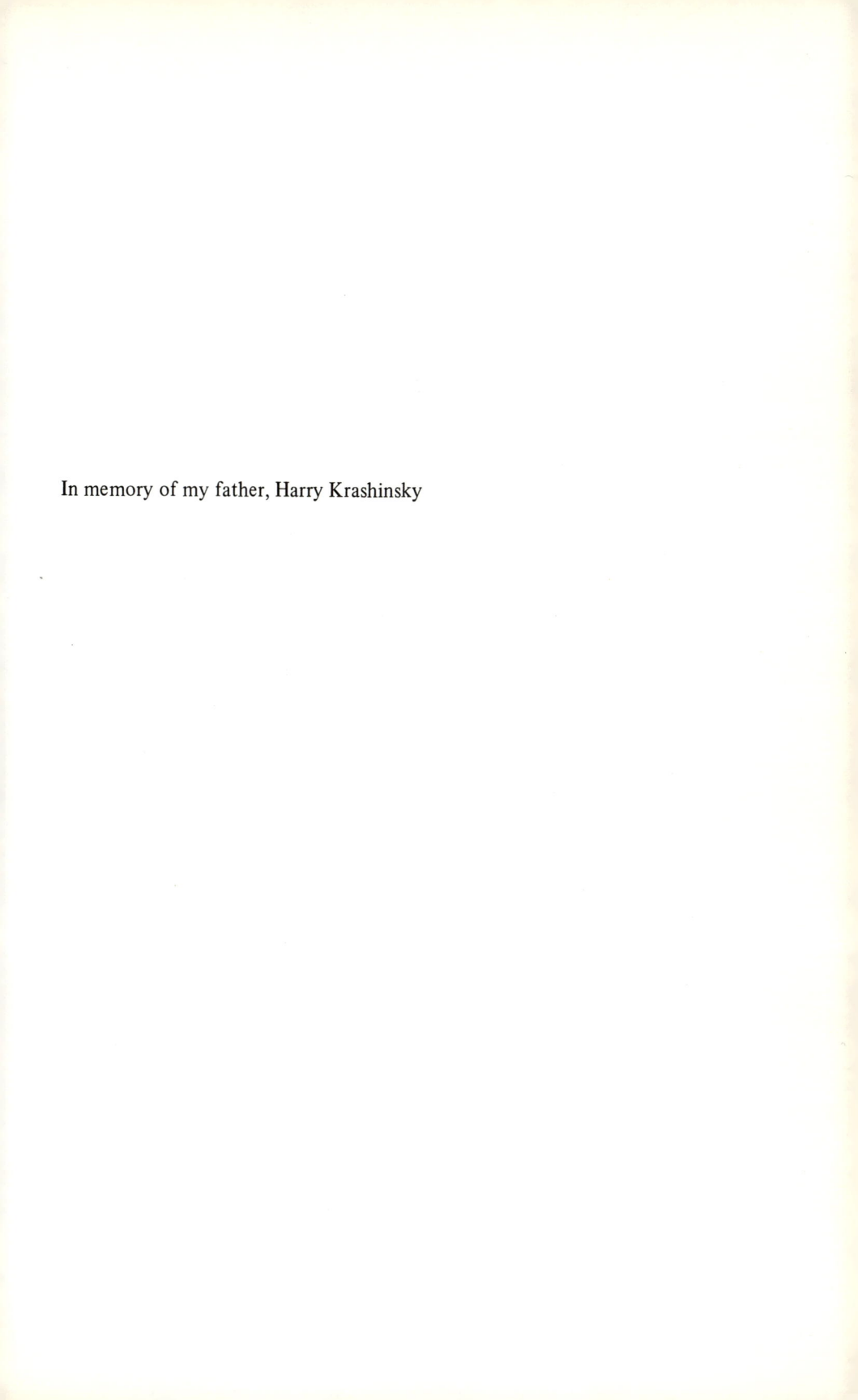

Contents

PREFACE ix

1
Introduction 3

2
Previous theories of cash vs in-kind transfers 9

3
Needs, inabilities, and a new economic theory of in-kind transfers 27

4
Some practical problems in in-kind programs 46

5
Some social service programs in Ontario 74

6
Conclusions 113

APPENDICES
A Traditional models of cash and in-kind transfers 117
B A simple model of overuse and inability 121
C A model of inability and cash and in-kind transfers 123
D Computer simulations of inability and optimal subsidies 134

viii Contents

E Principles for subsidy systems: suggestions by a federal-provincial working party 148
F Computer simulations targeting a subsidy for inability and/or low income 151

BIBLIOGRAPHY 158

Preface

I would like to thank the Ontario Economic Council for its help while this report was researched and written. Its financial assistance, moral support, and practical advice made possible the collecting of information and smoothed the writing process. In particular, Michael Mendelson and Lorie Tarshis read the manuscript carefully and made many useful suggestions. They provided encouragement and were always willing to discuss ideas as they emerged.

The final draft of this manuscript was written while I was on leave. I would like to thank the Social Science and Humanities Research Council of Canada for its financial support during that period. As well, I would like to thank the Institution for Social and Policy Studies at Yale University, which housed me and offered its assistance during my leave.

Many others were instrumental in the writing of this report. I wish to express my gratitude to the anonymous referees who made extensive comments on various drafts. My colleagues at Scarborough College of the University of Toronto made useful suggestions and provided a sympathetic audience as my ideas emerged; in particular, John Scadding and Meyer Bucovetsky were most attentive. At the Institute for Policy Analysis, Les Cseh was a co-operative and skilled computer programmer, and Mary Crossan did a careful job in typing the various drafts. Susan Rahn, my research assistant, interviewed a large number of the public employees cited in this book. Of course, I must also thank the many people working in the social services who were most generous with their time. Special thanks must go to Lenore d'Anjou, who was a careful and sensitive editor.

Naturally, I bear full responsibility for any errors or omissions in this report.

Finally, my gratitude goes to my wife, Katharine. She has provided constant encouragement and careful proofreading, and her patience and common sense sustained me through research, writing, and rewriting over the course of almost four years.

USER CHARGES IN THE SOCIAL SERVICES:
AN ECONOMIC THEORY OF NEED AND INABILITY

1
Introduction

When two groups of thoughtful, intelligent people persist in proposing diametrically opposed solutions to a problem, it is worth re-examining the terms of their arguments to discover whether they are talking about the same things. When one of the groups consists of economists, who deal in abstractions of reality, such re-examination is particularly appropriate. Do the models in question truly reflect all important facets of the world perceived by social planners and policy-makers? If not, the models tend to be irrelevant to planners' concerns, and economists forfeit their role of distinguishing good programs from those that ought to be scrapped.

This impasse seems to be the current situation in the social services. Social-planning conferences at all levels of government routinely include economists, but they have had curiously little impact on policy. This is particularly true with regard to subsidy programs and the debate on if, when, and how they should impose user charges.

The difficulty seems to be the means, not the goal. Policy-makers design their subsidy programs and consider user changes as parts of antipoverty strategy, an attempt to achieve more equality among individuals than would exist in a completely free market. Economists certainly agree that such an achievement would be desirable, but most — with a few recent exceptions — simply damn subsidy programs wholesale, saying very little about user charges in particular.

Their reason for doing so lies in economic theory. Logically, any discussion of user charges presupposes that there may be instances in which it is thinkable, even desirable, to set them below the cost of the service or even at zero — in other words, to provide a goods-specific subsidy for some or all users. Economists, however, generally disapprove of goods-specific subsidies. Traditional theory states that, with some very limited exceptions, efficiency can be achieved only when users pay the full costs of the goods and services they consume; if users are

4 User charges in the social services

too poor to pay these costs, that problem must be handled separately through income redistribution by some sort of negative income tax or other cash transfers. This preference extends to the delivery of social services provided by or through the government. Except in a few circumstances, economists generally recommend giving the poor cash with which they may choose to purchase a product through payment of a user charge equal to the full cost of the service. Policy-makers have ignored this dictum with great regularity and developed programs involving many kinds of goods-specific subsidies. Most economists respond by insisting that such programs exist only because of ignorance or political manipulation by special interests; for them, the theory remains intact. Since they believe almost no subsidies are sensible, they see little point in discussing user charges that are not equal to full cost.

Some theoricians have taken a different tack. Policy-makers' continued interest in subsidies, they say, suggests that the traditional economic models may not reflect all the pertinent factors of reality. So they invent elaborate justifications for existing programs. Unfortunately, these explanations have little relationship to what government officials and social scientists see as the reasons for the programs.

Both approaches are unproductive. Insisting that all subsidies are economic evils and that hundreds of apparently serious policy-makers are either ignorant or venal becomes unconvincing after a while. Failing to speak to their concerns is not much better. In effect, economists have eliminated themselves from useful discussion of many public programs.

This book is an attempt to enter the debate in an effective way. It offers a theory that justifies some — but by no means all — goods-specific subsidies. It has particular application to the social services because it takes account of a concept of inability and need that is related to social planners' concerns.[1] This theory enables the differentiation of economically good subsidy programs from poor ones. Moreover, it provides a number of practical insights into user changes. For example, it demonstrates that what may appear to be arbitrary and inefficient restrictions on who is eligible to receive a subsidy are often the *inevitable* result of targeting benefits to those who need them most. It also shows that user charges are most efficient when designed according to the intended recipients, rather than according to commodities, and consequently that different recipients

---

1 'Inability' will be defined precisely in Chapter 3. Basically, the term is used to describe a shift in the household production function that increases the inputs necessary to produce the characteristics (such as housekeeping, mobility, food preparation, recreation, child raising, and so on) consumed by the family. Inability is related to 'need' in ways discussed in Chapter 3.

may properly face quite differently structured charges for the same goods or services.

It is worth noting that this attempt to bridge the present gap between economists and social planners is not a mere academic exercise. Goods-specific subsidy programs abound in Canada, and there is much current interest in imposing or raising user charges for them.

This interest has two main sources. First, to many policy-makers, user charges seem to be an answer to an increasing dilemma. Although Ontario's expenditures on social services are by no means low (see Table 1), advocacy groups demand much more.[2] Simultaneously, however, taxpayers all over North America seem to have become disenchanted with large public expenditures. Some jurisdictions have even had to reduce government services. Policy-makers are caught between the two demands. Many see attaching or raising user charges to social services as a politically attractive way to maintain or expand programs. By doing so, they hope to satisfy the demands of activists and still be able to argue that taxpayers are bearing a reduced share of the costs.

The second reason for the current interest in user charges is related to this political reality, as well as to the recent history of Canadian social services. The mid-1960s saw a renegotiation of previous federal-provincial agreements on income maintenance and assistance to the poor. In 1966, the federal government passed the Canada Assistance Plan (CAP), under which Ottawa reimburses the provinces for 50 per cent of their expenditures on social services that meet certain criteria. The guidelines limit user charges and restrict assistance to persons in need or likely to be in need (which means, in practice, to those likely to be on welfare if the subsidized service is not available).

The CAP grants are open ended (in other words, there is no upper limit to the cost sharing), and they can be channelled to municipal governments in provinces, such as Ontario, that provide many social services at the local level. Since the availability of CAP, Ontario has reimbursed 80 per cent of municipal expenditures on programs eligible for federal support.

Not surprisingly, the availability of 'fifty-cent dollars' has led to a dramatic expansion of the social services at the provincial level. Ontario municipalities, given a chance to provide programs for which they pay only 20 per cent of cost, have acted with equal enthusiasm.

2 For example, some activists propose universal free day care as the solution for a number of social problems affecting preschool children. In 1974-5, such a program would have cost upwards of $3 billion − more than four times the entire budget of the Ministry of Community and Social Services for that year and about two hundred times the province's actual expenditures on day care (Ontario Public Accounts 1974-5, 143-64).

TABLE 1
Ministry of Community and Social Services grants, subsidies, etc., 1976-7

Demonstration projects approved in council				$ 481,741
Grants to agencies				599,489
Income maintenance				
Provincial allowances and benefits			$342,804,625	
Support for municipal costs, allowances and benefits			133,979,530	
Drug benefit plan			12,721,574	
Training allowances and expenses			8,230,921	
Rehabilitation services for the disabled			988,396	
Residential programs (workshops and work activity)	—	Capital	670,971	
	—	Operating	7,564,930	$506,960,947
Social services				
Services for children				
Child welfare (children's aid societies)			$75,934,692	
Community and social services			1,310,649	
Children's and youth institutions			5,979,711	
Day nurseries			24,733,874	
Capital grants for facilities			3,137,426	$111,096,352
Facilities and programs for senior citizens				
Charitable institutions	—	Capital	1,573,750	
	—	Operating	17,018,940	
Homes for aged and rest homes	—	Capital	6,013,227	
	—	Operating	76,645,858	
Senior citizens' centres	—	Capital	497,559	
	—	Operating	1,264,868	
Community and social services	—	Capital	171,000	
	—	Operating	3,072,960	
Volunteer program for seniors			44,568	$106,302,730

Counselling and other supportive social services			
Homemakers and nurses services	4,959,250		
Credit counselling	510,501		
Family service agencies	458,857		
Assessment, restorative and therapeutic services	31,036		
Family crisis intervention	33,037	$ 5,992,681	$223,391,763
Community programs (generally for the retarded)			
Residential facilities and community resource centres	— Capital	1,368,943	
	— Operating	22,253,218	
Developmental, protective and other supportive services	— Capital	2,298,523	
	— Operating	14,656,849	
Ontario association for the mentally retarded		60,900	
Lorimer Lodge		22,700	$ 40,661,135
Payments in lieu of municipal taxes			333,750
		Total	$772,428,825

NOTE: Total ministry expenditures for the year were $947,099,328. This amount included $143,539,153 for wages, salaries, and benefits; $30,816,700 for travel, materials, and supplies; and $314,650 for the Social Assistance Review Board, in addition to the sums spent on grants and subsidies as detailed above. Source for all figures: Ontario Public Accounts, 1976-7.

8 User charges in the social services

Ottawa may or may not have foreseen the extent of the response to CAP. In the past five years, however, the federal government has indicated a desire to alter the open-ended arrangement and has held discussions with the provinces on how best to change CAP. One bill, C-57, which was proposed in 1975, would have increased the services eligible for cost sharing but designated some as available to all, regardless of income, and allowed lower user charges than CAP permits. Provincial opposition to the degree of federal control explicit and implicit in C-57 killed the proposal, but not before Ontario developed a number of demonstration projects with user charges in line with its schedules.

The changes in federal governments in 1979 and 1980 prevented passage of any other replacement for CAP, but it is clear that one will be sought and that it is likely to include provision for quite generous user charges. Whatever its specific arrangements, it will occasion revamping of antipoverty programs all over the country.

Accordingly, the time is ripe for economists to incorporate the social planners' realities into their models and so regain the ability to draw useful distinctions between good programs and bad and to make meaningful contributions to the design of user charges.

This book is one attempt to do so. Chapter 2 explores existing economic theories of goods-specific subsidies and explains which are acceptable and which inadequate. Chapter 3 develops the concept of inability used in this book and draws analogies from private insurance markets; the theory is described here in terms accessible to the noneconomist, with mathematical analysis and computer simulations presented in appendices. Chapter 4 applies this theory and acceptable older ones to an investigation of various methods used to vary program designs and user charges so as to deliver services to target groups and to reduce inefficiency. Questions of incentives and the integration of programs are also considered.

Chapter 5 applies the theory to specific social service programs in Ontario, showing how it can help the economist to understand them and the planner to construct user charges that are both economically sound and supportive of a program's particular goals. It begins with a detailed examination of two major social services, day care for young children and institutional care for the aged, and then considers a number of other services more briefly. Chapter 6 summarizes the conclusions of the book.

2
Previous theories of cash vs in-kind transfers

Before an economist can pass judgment on the utility of user charges, much less comment on their structure, he must question whether it is better for the government to help the socially disadvantaged by means of in-kind transfers (with or without user charges) or by cash transfers.

Such a discussion may strike noneconomists as somewhat circuitous. Social policy-makers in particular are oriented to getting things done; they tend to focus on immediate reality and find tedium in the step-by-step, all-encompassing abstractions of economics.

As human beings, economists are equally interested in accomplishment. Their science, however, deals in theory and abstractions because that is the only way they can express the complexity resulting from the millions of economic decisions made by individuals every day. Thus, when they discuss a mechanism such as user chargers, they must examine how it affects the models they have abstracted from the real world.

Working with abstractions keeps the economist aware of the need for strict definitions and thus of the differences that may exist among apparently similar things. Antipoverty programs are a case in point. The poor need goods and services they cannot afford to purchase; society, through the government (or through private charities, for that matter), can remedy the problem in several ways. It can give them the commodities in kind, it can give them enough cash to purchase the same commodities, or it can reimburse them after they have made such purchases. Since all these approaches are aimed at providing the same goods, the noneconomist may assume their price tags are similar. He is likely to prefer one or the other for practical reasons (administrative costs or simplicity), political attractiveness, or philosophical points (equity, the good of society).

The economist, however, looks at the methods of providing the commodities and distinguishes sharply between in-kind transfers and cash transfers. He also notes that reimbursement is simply one way of accomplishing an in-kind transfer and that a user charge below full cost is another; both involve providing the recipient with a subsidy for a specific good or service, usually in a specified amount.[1] A cash transfer, on the other hand, provides money to the recipient, who chooses how much of which good to purchase with it.

Having made this basic distinction, the economist examines the operation of both kinds of transfers within his model of abstracted reality. One of his goals is always seeing what action leads to the greatest economic efficiency, which he defines as a situation in which no rearrangement of inputs or outputs can make some members of society better off without hurting others. He starts with a fairly simple abstraction and then counts in factors to reflect various situations and complexities.

Two reasons may account for any differences between his conclusions and those of the more pragmatic social policy-maker. The latter undoubtedly wants economic efficiency, but he may put a higher priority on other, noneconomic goals. When this is the case, the economist can say little. Economic models cannot express some social concepts. If policy-makers prefer these concerns to the point of adopting inefficient, expensive programs to accommodate them, that concerns the economist only as a taxpayer, not as a professional.

On the other hand, the economist may not have included all pertinent factors in his model. He may even have omitted some that strike the layperson as too obvious to mention.

Both situations seem to exist in the long-standing debate over cash vs in-kind transfers. The economists' basic model shows that cash transfers are clearly preferable. The introduction of certain complicating realities does justify in-kind transfers, but the situations to which these factors apply are very limited. Meanwhile, policy-makers continue to design and promote in-kind programs for many other situations. Most economists have assumed the decision-makers were simply ignoring sound economic doctrine, either from ignorance or from a desire to pursue some noneconomic goal.

Recently, however, some economists have attempted to justify some of these programs by adding new considerations, some of which are not economic factors, into their models of reality. They have met with varied success, both in terms of economics and in terms of producing concepts (and results) that seem

---

1 Hence the term 'goods-specific subsidy', which is used as a synonym for 'in-kind transfer' throughout this book. 'Subsidized good' and even just 'subsidy' are also used here as equivalents for 'in-kind transfer'.

Notice that a program providing vouchers for a commodity or restricted set of commodities (such as the food stamp program in the United States) is yet another variation on an in-kind transfer.

to have any connection with the real world as it is perceived by the policy-makers. They have not changed the basic economic preference for cash transfers; neither have they produced an adequate justification for most of the in-kind programs that policy-makers prefer.

This chapter examines the existing theories of in-kind transfers, starting with the most basic, and comments on why some are useful, some inappropriate. It also suggests that introducing noneconomic or quasi-economic considerations has not worked, and that so far there has been no sound challenge to traditional theory, with its very limited justification of in-kind transfers.

THE SIMPLE MODEL OF CASH AND IN-KIND TRANSFERS

By definition, antipoverty programs are concerned with ensuring that each member of society has what he or she needs to achieve some minimum level of well-being. If an individual does not have sufficient means to obtain the goods and services required to reach this level, government social services use tax funds to transfer to him either the commodities themselves or the amount of cash needed to purchase them.

When an individual requires additional inputs to meet the designated level of well-being, economists generally regard in-kind transfers as inferior to direct cash transfers.[2] The model they use to reach this conclusion has intimidated many first-year economics students (it is reproduced in Appendix A), but the theory is quite simple.

Suppose it is decided to raise the well-being of an individual who appears to need a specific commodity. Is it more efficient to subsidize the commodity (that is, to provide the recipient with it for a user charge that is less than its full cost) or to give him cash equal to the amount of the subsidy and then impose on him a user charge equal to the commodity's full cost?

Assuming that the goal is to raise the individual's welfare as measured by himself, that he can make competent economic decisions, and that his consumption decisions do not affect anyone else in the economy, the superiority of the cash transfer is easily demonstrated. Suppose that a particular commodity is subsidized. Now suppose that the amount the government spends on the subsidy

---

2 This is not true if the commodity is a public good (that is, a good consumed jointly by consumers that cannot be produced by clubs or teams because of high transactions costs). Then in-kind transfers (or user charges less than full cost) are appropriate because social benefits exceed private benefits (see note 15).

Many goods and services produced in the public sector, however, are consumed privately in economic terms (that is, they are used by individuals or family units). This is true of almost all the commodities discussed in this book.

12 User charges in the social services

is given to the consumer as a cash transfer. He can choose to purchase the same amount of the formerly subsidized commodity and so be no worse off than if the subsidy were still in effect. Frequently, however, he decides to consume less of the particular commodity, more of other goods, and is better off in his own eyes. Since the cash transfer costs the taxpayer the same amount as the subsidy and since it provides the recipient with at least as much and perhaps more well-being, it is clearly more desirable.

An example illustrates this proof. Suppose that a subsidy of 75 per cent on the purchase of some good S is given to a client, who proceeds to purchase $4000 worth of the commodity. He pays $1000, and the subsidy costs the government an additional $3000.[3] If, instead, the government simply transfers $3000 to the client, then he can still afford to purchase the $4000 worth of S, using the government's $3000 and the same $1000 of his own. However, since he is now faced with the full cost of S, he may well choose to consume less of it and use a part of the money to purchase other products. Since the client's choice is made freely, he decides to consume less S and more other goods only if he prefers the result (a concept known to economists as revealed preference). Thus, a cash transfer can make the client better off in his own eyes at the same cost to the government. Alternatively, a cash transfer of somewhat less than $3000 can leave the client just as well off as the $3000 subsidy.

To put the basic argument another way: in-kind transfers lead to overuse of the commodity and thus to increased costs for the taxpayers; hence they are inefficient.[4] The saving that can be achieved by a cash transfer measures the relative inefficiency of the subsidy; it is a percentage of the subsidy that increases with the elasticity of substitution between the subsidized good and other goods.[5] Of course, if the program restricts the quantity of the subsidized

---

3 Remember that the user charge and the subsidy must add up to full cost; both are often expressed as percentages. Thus a 75 per cent subsidy means that the client is provided the commodity at a user charge equal to 25 per cent of its full cost.

Note, too, that the arguments used here and elsewhere in the book (unless otherwise indicated) omit administration costs. It is generally agreed that they run higher for in-kind programs, especially if, as is often the case, recipients are income-tested.

4 Of course, this simplified argument ignores the optimal-taxation literature. For example, if a particular in-kind transfer induces a recipient to enter the labour force when a cash transfer would not, then the additional tax revenue accruing to the government from his salary may make that subsidy efficient (see Appendix A, note 1). The number of instances to which this approach applies, however, is very limited, and it can only justify relatively small subsidies.

5 The elasticity of substitution measures the responsiveness of consumer choice to changes in relative prices. The more the consumer reduces his consumption of S in response to a rise in its price, the larger is the elasticity of substitution.

good that may be purchased, inefficiency is reduced. With a very strict limit, the program may even become efficient or nearly so. At that point, however, the government must expect users to exert significant political pressure to expand supply.

Aaron and von Furstenberg's examination of various housing subsidies in the United States (1971) illustrated both inefficiency in these in-kind transfers and the effect of restricting quantity. Assuming an elasticity of substitution of 1.0 between housing and other goods, housing costs at 25 per cent of total income, and no limits on quantity, they demonstrated that inefficiency would be about 10 per cent for a 25 per cent subsidy, 24 per cent for a 50 per cent subsidy, and 45 per cent for a 75 per cent subsidy. However, because the programs restrict their subsidies to specific amounts of housing in public housing developments, the efficiency losses are actually much lower. Taking an average subsidy of 50 per cent, the authors concluded that its inefficiency is 10 per cent if the elasticity of substitution is 0.5 and only 3 per cent if the elasticity of substitution is 1.0. In other words, in the best case (an elasticity of 1.0), $1.00 spent on housing subsidies is equivalent to $0.97 spent on cash transfers.

Many other studies have measured the inefficiency of in-kind transfers. For example, in examining the U.S. food stamp program, Clarkson (1976) found an overall efficiency loss of 17 per cent. Including administrative costs, he showed that the government spent over $1.09 to deliver $1.00 in food stamps to recipients, who in turn valued each dollar's worth of subsidy at less than $0.83. Hu and Knaub (1976) also found that food stamps were inefficient.[6]

---

6 Barmack (1977) questioned both studies but argued that although consumers probably consumed no more food than they would have without the stamps, the program should still be condemned because its administration costs are much higher than those associated with cash transfers. Clarkson had used a Cobb Douglas utility function with an implied value of 1.0 for the elasticity of substitution; a lower value would have reduced the efficiency loss. Barmack argued that Clarkson also chose incorrect values for family income and that Hu and Knauf did not control for family size, an important consideration in the demand for food.

Galatin (1973) found that in 1970 many recipients of food stamps did not consider them equivalent to an equal cash transfer. Smeeding (1977) argued that food, housing, and medical care subsidies in the U.S. all involved significant inefficiencies. He took the extreme position that any excess of in-kind transfers (over what would have been purchased had the client received an equivalent cash transfer) should be considered useless. Since his approach unrealistically assumed that the elasticity of substitution is zero, his estimates (that the cash equivalent values of U.S. food, housing, and medical care subsidies are 88, 56, and 68 per cent respectively of their market value) should be taken only as the minimum cash equivalents of in-kind subsidies.

It is worth noting that these authors, like many of their confreres, have tended to focus on food and housing, the two major in-kind programs in the United States. The existence of these two large-scale programs may have influenced the direction of theory, leaving a relative vacuum in areas that only appear to be similar. For example, restrictions on consumption can be effective only if recipients have similar demands for the commodity. This is likely in the case of housing, but not in the social services, whose very nature suggests that demand is likely to vary widely among individuals eligible for a subsidy.

TRADITIONAL JUSTIFICATIONS FOR IN-KIND TRANSFERS

Incompetence and related problems
The basic argument for the superiority of cash transfers assumes that the recipient can make competent economic decisions. This assumption appears in economic models when society accepts an individual's measurement of his own welfare. In some cases, however, society does not accept an individual's view of his own best welfare.[7] It regards some or all of his economic decisions as incompetent and decides to intervene by dictating a number of them. If this occurs, the model changes dramatically (see Appendix A).

Before we examine this new situation, it should be emphasized that the economist does not use the term 'incompetent' in a legal or in a demeaning way. In economics, an incompetent consumer is one whose consumption goals are considered partly or completely inappropriate. He may be legally incompetent (a young child or a severely retarded person). Or he may simply be someone who, if given free choice, would select a bundle of goods that society considers to be of significantly less value than another bundle costing the same amount.[8]

In the simple model of a cash vs an in-kind transfer, the inefficiency of the latter derives from the fact that the client can achieve the same level of well-being with the cash as with the more costly subsidy. The two transfers give him somewhat different bundles of goods; the similarity of the well-being they bring depends upon his making competent economic decisions in spending the cash. Suppose, however, that society (as represented by policy-makers) does not agree that the bundle of goods and services on which a client wishes to spend the cash makes him as well off as would the subsidized bundle. Because of his incompetence, he would not select the latter freely. Therefore, if society believes its

7 In economic terminology, the incompetent individual and society do not agree on where the indifference curve lies (see Figure A.2).
8 Because society's values change, the groups considered incompetent may shift over time. For example, mildly retarded individuals used to be considered completely incompetent; more recently, many are proving capable of living in the community and making many of their own economic decisions.

values to be significantly better than those of the incompetent consumer, it is more efficient to transfer the goods to him in kind.[9]

For an example of the way in which incompetence justifies (that is, makes efficient) the provision of a subsidized good, suppose that the client is an alcoholic and the commodity society wishes to provide is food. If given cash, the client may prefer purchasing relatively little food so as to have more money left for the purchase of alcoholic beverages. But we know that if he were sound, he would prefer more nourishment and less alcohol. For his own good, we use a subsidy to induce him to purchase more food than he would otherwise. The same approach can be used to provide socially approved goods to others judged incompetent, such as drug addicts, the mentally retarded, and children.

The same paternalistic approach can be used when lack of information creates a sort of partial incompetence. An otherwise competent client may not be willing to pay the full cost of a commodity because he does not realize its true value. Consider various counselling services. Most consumers do not purchase counselling on a regular basis and are, therefore, unable to decide when it is necessary; moreover, individuals with financial, marital, or child-related problems may be initially resistant to counselling. In these and similar cases, paternalism may justify subsidies, even up to 100 per cent.

Some situations do not involve actual incompetence, but they affect the utility function in the same way. Two of the most obvious involve the politics of the family. So far, the discussion of well-being has assumed that the recipient is an individual, but in the social services the client is often a family of more than one member. Economic decisions then represent some aggregate of the preferences of the family's adults (who presumably take the welfare of the children into account in some way). Complicated relationships and bargaining within the family determine the relative weights given the preferences of individual members. In some cases, there is a significant difference between the weight given an individual and the weight society believes he or she should receive. Paternalism then justifies the use of in-kind transfers to correct inequalities within the family.

For example, society may want to channel more family resources to children than parents provide (either because they do not choose to do so or they lack the knowledge to do so properly). Hot school lunches, early education, summer

---

9 As already noted, actually handing the consumer the goods is not the only way to accomplish this in-kind transfer. A voucher system or a user charge below full cost has exactly the same effect. An alternate method, often used in cases of certain kinds of incompetence, is the minimum-purchase subsidy (the recipient must purchase at least a certain amount of the specified good or lose the entire subsidy).

camp programs, and so on assist children directly. To the extent that parents would be willing to provide these services anyway, such programs amount to cash transfers, but to the extent that parents would not provide adequate nutrition or stimulation, they are in-kind transfers to a specific group that could not be reached by cash transfers.

Now consider conflicts among adults in the family. Their resolution depends upon the relative power of family members. If social policy-makers do not accept that distribution of power, they may use paternalism to justify otherwise inefficient economic tools.[10] It is argued, for example, that women who do not work outside the home are at great disadvantage in the family. Decisions are weighted towards wage-earners; a working woman earns her own pay cheque, has more options, commands more respect in society and in her home, and consequently receives a larger weight in the aggregate of economic decisions (so goes the argument). Many women do not work because the relatively low wages available to them would net them little or nothing after paying for child care. If policy concludes that these women are inadequately represented in household decision-making, then helping them enter the work force by subsidizing day care may be a useful tool.[11]

From the economist's viewpoint, all these consumers — the selfish or unknowledgable parent, the family that distributes decision-making unjustly, the reluctant candidate for counselling, as well as the alcoholic, the drug user, and the retarded or senile person — fail to optimize their utility functions. Thus they can all be treated in a similar fashion. Once one determines that the individual's or family's economic values and hence decisions differ significantly from those of society, it is a simple matter (at least in theory) to use paternalism as a justification for controlling those decisions through in-kind transfers.

Determining which differences are significant does, however, raise serious moral questions about the intrusion of government into the lives of individuals and families. Finding answers to these problems is not primarily the realm of economists, though a number have worried about them. Even those well known as liberals, however, have concluded, sometimes reluctantly, that the government,

---

10 For example, it can be argued that family allowance cheques are made out to mothers so as to give them a small but independent source of funds. For this reason, some women's groups have opposed the recent reduction of family allowance payments and their supplementation by tax credits. Although the change is economically progressive, they believe it is socially harmful to reduce the amount of independent cash available to the mother.

11 It should be pointed out, however, that similar effects might be achieved by simply reducing the currently high rate of taxation on the earnings of the second wage-earner in the family. Such a scheme is suggested in Chapter 5 of this book.

acting for society, must sometimes step in. For example, Milton Friedman, in commenting on the difficulty of drawing a line between competence and incompetence, agreed that 'there is no avoiding the need for some measure of paternalism' (Friedman 1962, 33). Thurow saw less difficulty; he suggested that competence is simply a matter of degree and that in-kind transfers are a mild way of inducing individuals 'to make those decisions that society thinks they would be making if they were "competent"' (Thurow 1974, 193). He went on to suggest that consumers are not all equally efficient at managing their budgets; in that case, he said, equal cash transfers may give different consumers very different levels of well-being, and in-kind programs can minimize this inequality.[12]

Others have justified the intrusion of the state in the decision-making process of the individual or family as a form of social insurance. Does the voter support a particular form of paternalism even if it might affect *him* someday? If he were to become a destitute alcoholic, would he prefer the government to give him cash or to insist on providing food and lodging in kind? A decision made now, while he is presumably competent, may later protect him from himself.[13]

So the moral problems presented by paternalistic in-kind subsidies can be solved. The problem most pertinent to this book, however, is more difficult: the majority of the social service programs considered for subsidy serve clients who are economically competent. If these in-kind programs can be justified, it must be for reasons other than incompetence.

Conventional externalities

Another justification for in-kind transfers is even more straightforward than incompetence and offers no moral problems. This is the existence of positive externalities.

One of the assumptions of the basic model is that the benefits of consumption of the particular good accrue only to the recipient. But suppose that his consumption also benefits others in the economy. In this situation, the market

---

12 This argument has many points in common with the one developed in Chapter 3 of this book. Thurow, however, restricted himself to instances of economic incompetence; the model of inability in this book goes further.

13 Rawls argued that individuals can only decide upon a framework for society when they are in a hypothetical state of equal liberty, where 'no-one knows his place in society, his class position or social status, nor does anyone know his fortune in the distribution of natural assets and abilities, his intelligence, strength, and the like' (Rawls 1971, 12).

Mishan suggested the economic equivalent: that agreement be reached 'on a tolerable structure of disposable incomes and, therefore, of the patterns of transfers necessary to implement it' only in a 'hypothetical state' in which no one knows his exact position in the income distribution (Mishan 1972, 976).

system does not fully account for all the benefits of consumption, and a cash transfer cannot ensure enough of the good being consumed. So when externalities are present, efficiency generally requires a subsidy to the purchase of the good; then its price (including the subsidy) includes the external effect of consumption, and it induces the consumer to act as if he had the welfare of others in mind.

Some examples may clarify this concept. Consider the area of public health. If one person's expenditure on health care in turn benefits others (say, by reducing the chance of infection), then an externality exists. The individual, considering only his own welfare, may not be willing to pay the full cost of the services he must have if the people around him are to obtain the benefits of his consumption. Accordingly, public health services ought to be subsidized so as to induce him to use enough of them.

Alternately, consider education. If one accepts the idea that the education of poor children improves their citizenship and thus the quality of life (political and otherwise) in the community, this constitutes an argument for subsidy. In the social services, day care provides developmental and educational services for young children. If children who are poorly cared for grow up to impose a burden on the rest of society (by committing crimes or simply by being irresponsible citizens and neighbours), then subsidies to developmental programs can be justified.[14]

When an externality is present, the subsidy required for efficiency may be substantial. As a percentage of the price of the commodity, it must be equal to that percentage of the benefits that accrue to others besides the purchaser. Thus, if my consumption of a unit of S results in an increase in utility or well-being for myself and each of 99 other consumers, and if each of us places the same dollar value on that increase, then I should receive a 99 per cent subsidy.[15]

The theory of externalities, like that of incompetence, is widely accepted in economics; where applicable, it clearly justifies the use of in-kind transfers.

14 It might also be argued that better day care and education make it more likely that poor children will become productive, tax-paying members of society, thus reducing the burden on other taxpayers. If correct, this argument, while not offering a nonpecuniary externality, suggests that welfare dollars are more efficiently spent on the young than on adults. In some ways, this is an optimal taxation argument, applied over time.
15 If the externality is significant, the good begins to resemble a public good and is generally produced by the government under well-known, if hard-to-apply, economic rules (see, for example, Samuelson 1954). Theoretically, if transaction costs are low, the parties involved can arrange deals among themselves that avoid the need for public involvement. Unfortunately, transaction costs are seldom low: in small groups, strategic behaviour raises bargaining costs; in large groups, sheer numbers and the problem of 'free riders' make optimal arrangements difficult to achieve privately.

Unfortunately, it is not applicable in many of the areas where social planners discern a need for in-kind transfers. Many of these involve goods and services that are primarily private, commodities whose consumption benefits accrue mostly to the consumer.

Food is clearly a private good, as is housing (except to the extent to which run-down housing offends other people). Medical care, excepting the treatment and prevention of contagious diseases, primarily benefits the recipient and his family. The benefits of social services, such as visiting homemakers and nurses and services for the handicapped and the aged, all accrue to the individuals or families receiving the service. The same is true of day care, to the extent that the care is simply custodial.

If any economic justification exists for providing these programs through subsidies, we shall have to look further to find it.

NEWER ATTEMPTS TO JUSTIFY IN-KIND TRANSFERS

Donor preferences
In recent years, some economists have attempted to justify many in-kind social service programs by using the notion of donor preferences. The theory extends the conventional externalities approach to poor individuals' consumption of private goods. It runs something like this: taxpayers (donors) prefer that the poor consume certain goods (for example, food, housing, clothing, and medical care) rather than others (for example, fast cars, alcohol, and drugs); therefore, overall welfare is increased by using in-kind transfers to modify the poor's consumption choices. In other words, say proponents of the theory, in-kind transfers of the correct size leave both rich and poor better off than do cash transfers.

This approach may have had its origins in an article by Hochman and Rodgers (1969) which concluded that increasing the incomes of poor consumers also provides direct benefits to the rich. Although their argument was directed to justifying income redistribution, once one accepts the inclusion of the income of the poor in the donor's utility function, it is a relatively minor step to include the consumption of particular goods and hence in-kind transfers. A number of authors who have made this assumption have concluded that it is efficient to subsidize the poor's consumption of those commodities valued by donors.[16]

Daly and Giertz gave the gist of the donor preference theory by commenting: 'the ultimate motivation for nonrecipient support of public welfare schemes may lie precisely in the ability of those plans to influence consumption patterns

---

16 See, for example, Garfinkel 1973, Giertz and Sullivan 1977, and Yandle 1974. For some of the earlier literature in this area, see Pauly (1970) and Buchanan (1968).

... For donors the crucial issue may be not the level of well being achieved by the recipient but rather *how* he achieves it.' (Daly and Giertz 1972, 136)

The noneconomist may label this view paternalistic, but the paternalism described and accepted earlier in this chapter is something altogether different from donor preferences. Traditional economic paternalism means that if the recipient of a subsidy knew what the policy-maker (or taxpayer) knows, he would alter his consumption package. To put it another way, if the taxpayer, knowing what he knows, were in the recipient's position, he would voluntarily consume the good in question and consider himself better off for having done so. If the recipient is not permanently and completely incompetent, he can be educated to want to consume the subsidized good.

Donor preferences, on the other hand, do not mean that the recipient is incompetent or in any way does not know his own best interests. The notion suggests improving the taxpayers' welfare by altering the recipient's consumption pattern; this alteration makes the recipient worse off in his own eyes and no amount of education or competence can convince him otherwise. If the taxpayer, knowing what he knows, were in the recipient's position, he would choose the same bundle of goods as the recipient does. Consuming more of the good for which a subsidy is proposed does not make him (the taxpayer in the recipient's shoes) better off.

Here we see the chief philosophical argument against the donor preference theory. Mishan has argued that no form of redistribution should depend on donor preferences, that 'just as externalities arising from envy or malice may not be agenda for society, so neither may be externalities arising from benevolence' (Mishan, 1972, 976). In other words, donor preferences may exist, but our concept of privacy should prevent our entering them into public policy, whether or not the individuals concerned are wealthy. For example, if donors preferred the poor to 'use' more religious services, programs could be designed to provide income to those who attend church regularly. But even if the recipients did not object to this type of program, we would consider it inappropriate for a public body (though not necessarily for a charitable organization).

Several more theoretical objections can also be raised to justification by donor preference. First, the theory can explain only a limited amount of redistribution, a problem also suggested by Musgrave (1970). Relatively small transfers achieve a point at which further redistribution would hurt some individuals and destroy efficiency.[17]

---

17 Suppose that there are only two consumers, one rich and one poor, and that the rich consumer's utility depends not only on his own income but also on the poor person's income. For simplicity suppose that each person receives utility from his own income

Second, the donor preference theory makes the unusual assumption that consumption choices of the poor enter the utility function of the rich, but not the other way around. Yet surely the rich's 'overconsumption' of fancy cars, furs, and jewellery may affect the poor, just as the poor's 'underconsumption' of food or housing is assumed to affect the rich. Or perhaps the assumption is that being a taxpayer entitles one to meddle in the consumption decisions of the poor. But why then does being a welfare recipient not entitle one to any say in the consumption of the rich? Once this particular floodgate is opened, few commodities would be free from government involvement.

Third, one has only to enter freedom into the utility function of the poor to outweigh the effect of donor preferences. If the poor care about being denied full responsibility for their own consumption (and this is no more abstract than caring about the amount your neighbour spends on cars rather than food), then they may be worse off in an in-kind program than in a cash-transfer program, even if their consumption is the same in each case. If it is reasonable that the rich be entitled to care about the format of income redistribution, it is no less reasonable to allow the poor to do so.

These objections are often countered with the statement that whether or not one likes donor preferences, that is the way people vote. This is scarcely an answer. It would mean that any subsidy program could be justified *ex post facto* by stating that, after all, voters prefer the poor (or any consumers) to have somewhat more of the good than the recipients themselves might choose.

A theory that can explain everything explains nothing. If any set of preferences is legitimate, then any argument can justify policy. Two examples illustrate this point. First, in the United States, where food stamps are a major in-kind program, writers have suggested that minimum standards for nutrition are a natural goal for donors. Yet in other western countries where in-kind programs abound, food stamps are conspicuously absent, although one expects that the preferences of middle-class taxpayers do not change radically with national boundaries. Second, when Ontario's Family Benefits and the American Aid to Families with Dependent Children programs were first introduced, their

---

equal to I^a where I is income and a is some power, and that the rich person values the poor person at a fraction β of himself. For simplicity, we can write the rich person's utility function as $U(I_r, I_p) = I_r^a + \beta I_p^a$, where I_r and I_p are the incomes of the rich and poor respectively. If a = 0.5, then the rich person welcomes redistribution only if $I_r/I_p > 1/\beta^2$. Thus, if β = 0.5, the rich person would have to have more than four times the income of the poor before he would welcome redistribution (which would occur until $I_r = 4I_p$). If β = 0.25, redistribution would be efficient only if $I_r/I_p > 16$!

proponents explained their high implicit marginal tax rates[18] on earned income by suggesting that donors preferred to have welfare mothers stay at home than to work. But shortly afterwards, day-care programs became very popular, and the same experts announced that taxpayers, convinced of the work ethic, wanted mothers out in the labour force. When preferences seem to jump about so abruptly, the theory becomes less than useful.

The moral is clearly that, on philosophical, theoretical, and logical grounds, economists should leave politics to the politicians. If a policy-maker chooses to support a policy because he thinks his constituents want it, there is no point in supplying him with unsound economic theory to support it. If the policy-maker is later voted out of office because taxes have gone up to pay for inefficient programs and taxpayers see no reduction in poverty, then he has no one to blame but himself for misjudging public opinion over the long term.

Economic rights

A number of economists have suggested that in some markets one might not allow consumer sovereignty to rule, and that consumers, whatever their incomes, ought to have the right to some minimum supply of certain goods. Tobin calls this belief 'specific egalitarianism', in the sense that we might 'somehow remove the necessities of life and health from the prizes that serve as incentives for economic activity, and instead let people strive and compete for non-essential luxuries and amenities' (Tobin 1970, 265-6).

Okun also suggested that society limits the market because of a sense that certain transactions (for example, selling one's children into slavery) flow only from extreme duress. Of course, he noted, these limits are meaningless unless we ensure that everyone has sufficient funds to avoid such situations. Finally, Thurow argued that every member of society has a right to certain minimum amounts of certain commodities. For example, he said, medical care guarantees one's right to life, while education and housing are included in our sense of what constitutes a good society; guaranteeing minimums of such essential commodities increases individuals' shares in the common values essential for the continuation of society (Thurow 1974, 192-4).

These arguments seem persuasive, but the economic question remains: why must in-kind transfers be used to guarantee minimum amounts of basic commodities?

---

18 A marginal tax rate need have nothing to do with the tax system *per se*. When program benefits are reduced as income rises, the reduction acts as an implicit tax or tax-back. For example, suppose that program benefits are reduced by 75 per cent of any increase in the recipient's income. If he earns an extra $1.00, his benefits fall by $0.75, so his net income rises by only $0.25. This benefit reduction clearly acts as a 75 per cent tax.

Would it not be more efficient for society to use cash transfers to provide sufficient funds for all consumers to purchase what is their right?

Tobin rejects both food stamps and subsidized housing in favour of cash transfers (Tobin 1970, 276). In his prime examples, education and medical care, justifying subsidies depends on highly inelastic supply and a desire for equal opportunity for the young. Many of the social services require other explanations of why cash transfers may not always be the efficient way to guarantee universal access to minimum levels of certain goods.

Political Realities

Attempts to mix economics and politics usually fail; nevertheless some economists support subsidized social services not as a means of helping the poor that is economically efficient but as one that is politically possible. Thus, they admit that general income redistribution via a negative income tax would yield the greatest all-round social welfare. But politics may make such a program difficult to achieve. Therefore, they say, progressive citizens should work for in-kind transfers to the poor as the best feasible alternative.

A similar argument promotes improving income distribution through in-kind transfers that reach a large proportion of the population (for example, hot-lunch programs in the United States and government-subsidized medical insurance in Canada). Only such general programs, say the believers, can generate the broad political support needed to get any antipoverty legislation passed.

These are not economic arguments, but their assumptions have entered some of the recent literature on public pricing. Feldstein (1972), LeGrand (1975), and Munk (1977) all justified subsidized prices for goods consumed by the poor; all did so in models that permitted no other redistribution.

It is hardly surprising that by ruling out income transfers, these authors were able to argue for distributional in-kind subsidies. Again one must ask, why rule out cash transfers? None of these writers has suggested a good reason why a negative income tax might not be used to redistribute income. There is much naïveté in arguing that the middle and upper classes can be fooled into redistribution through the price system when they would not support it directly through a tax-transfer system. If any group in the economy knows its own financial interests, it is the well-to-do. And if voters are willing to allocate a certain amount of money to redistribution, it is only good sense to use that money as efficiently as possible.

Moreover, the redistributional argument may actually be counterproductive. It assumes that subsidy programs can be financed by money that might otherwise be available for income transfers. However, Bird recently suggested the *possibility* that 'the tendency to introduce real or pseudo-distributional dimensions into every aspect of public finance may well result in *less* rather than more redistribution than would otherwise take place' (Bird 1976, 234). In effect, he argued that when a large part of the budget is used to finance inefficient redistributive programs (which are usually in-kind programs), then people 'learn' that redistribution is expensive and inefficient and are likely to vote for less redistribution of any kind. In other words, if the 'price' of redistributing one dollar to the poor rises, taxpayers may easily decide to 'purchase' less of it.[19]

The argument that broadly based programs are necessary to build the political coalition necessary for passage is also misconceived. It is hard to imagine that the well-to-do are going to vote eagerly for programs that cost them one dollar in taxes for every fifty cents they receive in benefits (which must be the case if the programs are to be redistributive). More likely, particular affluent taxpayers support specific broad-based programs that are structured to benefit them. For example, much of the support for extending day-care subsidies up the income scale comes from affluent working parents with young children, not from the affluent as a group. Similarly, middle and upper class university students have found a variety of reasons why raising university fees closer to full cost would be 'oppressive to the poor' despite the facts that the children of the poor are not well represented in university, and that most such proposals include generous scholarships that might well leave the poor students much better off than they are now).

THE INADEQUACY OF EXISTING THEORY

In summary, the existing economic theories on cash and in-kind transfers in the social services are inadequate. Some do not address many of the issues of concern to policy-makers; others are bad economics, usually because their proponents are working from noneconomic assumptions.

Conventional theory can make strong statements in some areas. Where there are no unusual circumstances, it shows the superiority of cash transfers, making a strong case for some sort of negative income tax as the basic safety net of any antipoverty program. Where there are obvious externalities, where recipients are clearly incompetent, where public programs are designed to reinforce or establish community values, it justifies in-kind programs nicely. Unfortunately, a

---

19 No evidence is possible to prove this, but the possibility should give pause to those supporting the introduction of distributional considerations into every aspect of public finance. If Bird's theory is true, it might partially explain the 'taxpayers' revolt' symbolized by the success in California of Proposition 13 limiting property taxes and government expenditures.

relatively small proportion of existing in-kind programs fall into these categories, and those that do tend not to be under attack. Few policy-makers or economists question the wisdom of public-health programs (justified by externalities, both in health and in information), the need to care for orphans, abused children, and the severely retarded (justified by the incompetence of the recipients), or publicly financed education (justified by externalities and the instilling of community values). Although there may be disagreement over the form of these programs — public vs private provision, direct transfers of commodities vs vouchers — there is little question of turning cash over to young students or the severely retarded.

Economists have treated other subsidy programs less well, even though they continue to proliferate. Conventional theory damns them. Other explanations, such as donor preferences, economic rights, and political expediency, are less satisfactory.

This is not to deny that the poor have inalienable rights or that taxpayers have various preferences and prejudices, but rather to suggest that the economist should leave such concerns to politicians and be content to analyze the effectiveness of various transfer programs in fighting poverty. What is frequently explained as donor preferences may well turn out to be donors' bad economics; taxpayers may support policies not because of donors' preferences but because they misjudge the policies' ultimate effects.

The same sort of caution applies to the 'accept-political-realities' argument. In evaluating welfare programs, it is not the economist's role to line up votes. He is most useful in explaining why various subsidies are ineffective and expensive and why there is no magic formula to end poverty. Noneconomists tend to mistrust the market and fear that unless essential goods are transferred to the poor directly, the rich will outbid them in their efforts to secure those goods in the market; policy-makers find it easy to underestimate the supply elasticity of most goods, an underestimate that is encouraged by special interest groups that stand to gain by specific programs. If the economist has explained economic facts to policy-makers and taxpayers, he has done his job, even if they then pursue inefficient policies for other reasons. To say that voters (or policy-makers) do what they want is tautological.

Nevertheless, economists who are examining antipoverty programs cannot say there is no need for new work in the area. Sound theory is not necessarily conventional theory, and conventional theory is not necessarily complete. All policy-makers are not the captives of political imperatives or special interest groups, yet they continue to propose subsidy programs for situations that conventional theory does not justify. Perhaps there really is a gap between the world they know and the one reflected in traditional economic models.

It is undoubtedly the desire to fill this gap that has led some of the modern economists cited in this chapter to their theories of donor preferences and political accommodation. Their failure to find an economically satisfying solution does not make their goal less worthy — or less urgent if economists are to make meaningful contributions to social policy planning. The problem is to discover the missing concepts and translate them into acceptable economic terms.

The first step may be listening to what social policy-makers are actually saying. When one actually discusses subsidy programs with them, one hears very little about the preferences of taxpayers. Rather they talk about meeting the needs of the poor and about helping them become self-sufficient, hardly the concerns of men and women who are merely trying to garner votes or even to 'salve the liberal conscience', as Giertz and Sullivan (1977, 34) have suggested. In some cases, the policy-makers may still be in error because they have underestimated the high costs of subsidy programs as compared with cash transfers. But in other instances, they may have identified needs that cannot be efficiently reached by cash transfers.

The word 'needs' occurs over and over again. In the next chapter, it is used as the take-off point for a new model that justifies a number of subsidy programs in the social services. It may assist the economist in identifying efficient and inefficient programs and in making meaningful recommendations.

3
Needs, inabilities, and a new economic theory of in-kind transfers

Recent failures to bridge the gap between economists and policy-makers do not suggest the attempt is unworthy. On the contrary, hard times and the prevalence of poverty make it ever more urgent for economists to find some way of talking the social planners' language, reflecting their concerns in economic models, and making believable economic statements about the efficiency with which taxpayers' money is used to help the poor.

'Talking the social planners' language' is not used here only as a catch phrase. Conversations with policy-makers show that although they do care about efficiency and about the desires of taxpayers, their primary thrust in social programs is defining and meeting the needs of various clients. The only economic models that can have much meaning for them are those that take account of this overriding concern.

Variation in need, of course, is a concept economists are usually reluctant to deal with; it involves interpersonal comparisons, which are difficult to reduce to abstractions. Yet only by using it can one develop a model of the world in which social planners work every day. And interestingly enough, once such a model is developed, it reveals that some – though by no means all – in-kind transfers are indeed justified and that user charges below full cost sometimes provide a convenient controlling mechanism.

The new theory developed in this chapter argues that in order to measure the assistance a family requires to escape poverty, the agency performing that measurement must know not only the family's income but also its needs. Where those needs can vary and where that variation is, for various reasons, hard to measure, in-kind transfers may be appropriate. A key concept is individual differences in ability to achieve the same degree of well-being with the same resources.

It must be emphasized that this theory in no way rejects the general superiority of cash transfers nor the mitigating circumstances of externalities and paternalism. Rather it is an attempt to expand the list of exceptions to the general case in a useful way. In doing so, it justifies a number of programs that seem to be covered inadequately by existing work.

The theory is at once normative and positive.[1] It is normative because it argues that under specified circumstances rather large in-kind transfers can be efficient, even in the absence of incompetence or externalities. (These transfers may be accomplished by providing subsidized goods and services with or without user charges below cost). It is positive because it deals with the real concerns of policy-makers and voters. Even if some economists are so unwilling to make interpersonal comparisons as to find the model's concept of inability theoretically unacceptable, anyone in touch with the real world has to admit that ability seems to play some significant role there and that it is implicit in many of the social welfare policies being evolved today.

This chapter explains the concepts of inability and need and argues that in-kind subsidies are desirable when different abilities cannot be easily identified for the purpose of varying cash transfers. (For the convenience of noneconomists, the theory is developed verbally in the text; the mathematical theory and computer simulations based on it are presented in Appendices C and D). The text then draws an analogy between the social services and private insurance markets, where benefits are often paid in-kind rather than in cash. The chapter concludes with some general comments on the roles of both in-kind and cash transfers in any welfare program.

THE CONCEPTS OF INABILITY AND NEED

For the economist, an individual achieves well-being by maximizing his utility function to the limitation of his income. In other words, he transforms his income into utility. What is not much discussed in economics is the fact that people differ in their ability to make this transformation. Yet the less able a given individual is to make it, the more income he needs to achieve any given level of well-being. Clearly then, an effective antipoverty program must consider *both* income and inability in determining what a client needs to escape poverty (reach some minimum level of utility).[2]

---

1 Normative models suggest which programs should be adopted, while positive models suggest which programs will be adopted by policy-makers.
2 Similarly, horizontal equity requires that both income and any inability be taken into account in determining an individual's tax liability. This is, in fact, the effect of deductions for medical expenses and for conditions such as age and physical disability.

Many social planners apparently see the need for this twofold consideration. They design income-maintenance programs in an attempt to protect individuals who suffer because their income is too low. But they also design in-kind programs in an attempt to protect individuals who suffer because they cannot achieve socially acceptable levels of well-being on incomes that might be perfectly adequate for other individuals.

In other words, persons whose utility functions are reduced (for whatever reason) require more income than average to achieve any given level of wellbeing. It remains to be seen whether in-kind transfers are an efficient means of compensating for low utility functions, but their existence must not be overlooked in modelling for antipoverty strategy.

Traditional economists do not entirely overlook the possibility of changes in the utility function — for example, they admit that various kinds of incompetence can change it enough to alter the general model significantly. The model in this book, however, assumes that competent consumers may differ in their ability to transform income into utility and hence in the inputs they need to achieve well-being.[3]

The use of the word 'need' signals the problem. 'Needs' are obviously related to 'demands' (in the economic sense of the word), but so are 'wants'. Theorists have been reluctant to deal with consumers' variations in needs because of the difficulty in distinguishing 'needs' from 'wants'. One person demands more clothing, another with the same income more medical care, a third more alcohol. Although their wants are obviously different, it is difficult to prove that one's needs are any greater than the others. It cannot be determined whether the scotch drinker derives more satisfaction from his consumption than does the wine drinker from his. Without making value judgements and comparing individual circumstances, it is equally impossible to know whether the consumption of clothing, medical care, or even alcohol leads to greater well-being.

Making such interpersonal comparisons is something economics has trouble coping with. Standard microeconomics does note individual differences in consumption choices and even derives individual demand curves. On any larger scale, however, it is difficult to account for individuals, so standard models aggregate demand and represent all individuals of a given income as a single consumer.[4] Conventional theory assumes that the price system allows each consumer to

---

3 This general approach is obviously not new in itself. For example, Arrow (1971) suggested that benefits enjoyed by consumers from government programs depend not only on the program but on the 'ability' of the consumer.
4 The same consumer stands for all households or families, adjusted to a common size.

cater to his or her own special tastes.[5] It gives no significance to variation in demand; for example, in comparing two consumers with the same income, it makes no comment on the relative well-being of one who spends more on automobiles and another who prefers clothing.

Recently, some economists have paid somewhat more attention to variations in demand. In discussing in-kind transfers as a means of redistribution, Feldstein (1975), LeGrand (1972), and Munk (1977) all raised the possibility that some groups of consumers may demand more of some commodities than do other groups. Interestingly, however, all three authors see this variation as caused by variations in income,[6] and their models use indirect utility functions that vary only with income and prices. Their explicit assumption is that two individuals (or households) faced with the same income and prices have the same level of utility. Yet this is precisely the assumption that seems to have little connection with the reality faced by the social services.

Weitzman recently took a different tack. He allowed consumers' needs to vary within each income class, assuming that 'any person in this population is endowed with a particular set of needs and a certain level of income. I am purposely using the loaded word 'need' instead of 'taste' or 'preference' to bring home the point that, for whatever reason, we are dealing with a commodity whose just distribution is considered a worthy end in itself' (Weitzman 1977, 518-19).

This begins to sound more to the point. But Weitzman distributed the marginal utility of income so that it was independent of need,[7] and he showed no other reason why the commodity examined should be one whose just distribution is a concern for public policy. In his model, consumers with higher need obtain greater utility from the same income than consumers with lower need, so their greater consumption hardly seems a pressing social issue. Moreover, Weitzman was comparing the price system to rationing, which is very different from the in-kind transfers that are the concern of this study. In-kind transfers in the social services are generally geared to delivering more of a commodity to those

---

5 In a way, it is the inability of policy-makers to predict tastes and hence consumption that makes cash transfers superior to in-kind transfers in the general model.
6 LeGrand discussed the provision of subsidies to low income groups, while Feldstein and Munk discussed the 'distributional characteristic' of a good (Feldstein 1972, 33) in terms of the income elasticity of demand, although their models may all be reinterpreted in terms of other variations.
7 Weitzman's utility function is $U = C + (A + \epsilon) x/B + x^2/2B$, where A, B, and C are constants, x is the quantity of the good purchased, and ϵ is the need of the individual. As ϵ rises, so does utility.

A new theory of in-kind transfers 31

whose needs are larger, something rationing does not do in Weitzman's model.[8] Furthermore, in-kind transfers generally concern goods and services that are seldom in inelastic supply and rarely preclude wealthier consumers from purchasing more of them; rationing, on the other hand, restricts each consumer, wealthy or not, needy or not, to the same level of consumption.

Few social policy-makers could disagree with the idea that some consumers have greater needs than do others in the same income class. If the concept is to be useful in an economic discussion, however, it is necessary to go one step further and relate it to utility. That extra step, which may strike sociologists as completely obvious, is the key to my model, so it must be spelled out carefully: when income is held constant, consumers with greater needs have lower levels of utility. To put it another way, the greater an individual's need, the more income he acquires to achieve a given level of utility. For example, a disabled person has greater needs than an average person who is not disabled; if both are to achieve the same well-being (level of utility), the former requires more income.

For the economist, the problem with this formulation is the term 'need'. As we have seen, individuals want many different items; how does one separate the differences in their needs from the differences in their tastes?

The problem can be resolved theoretically by using a model developed by Lancaster (1966). In the usual utility function employed by economists, the individual's utility depends upon the goods and services he purchases in the market. Lancaster argued that this concept conceals the production that takes place within the household. In his model, consumption is a two-stage process: the consumer purchases goods and services; he then uses his expertise and time to combine these purchases to produce 'characteristics'. (For example, he combines purchased food, electricity, and a kitchen to produce 'supper'.) His utility then depends upon these characteristics.

Extrapolating from Lancaster's concept, it is clear that any two consumers may differ in their ability to transform what they purchase into characteristics. Less ability − in other words, inability − implies that an individual requires more inputs than average to produce any given level of outputs (characteristics). Thus, prices and income limit the various bundles of goods a consumer can purchase, and these bundles plus his household production functions, which vary

8 Using $\bar{x}$ as the average amount of the good available in society and ϵ as the need of an individual (defined so that ϵ is distributed in the population with mean zero and so that an individual's demand is equal to ϵ plus the average demand of his income class), Weitzman defined $\bar{x} + \epsilon$ as the optimal distribution of the good. Comparing the price system and rationing, he concluded that the price system will come closer to the optimum when income is uneven but needs are more uniform. (Weitzman 1977, 519-23). This is not a surprising result given his definition of optimal distribution.

according to ability, limit the various combinations of characteristics within the set it is feasible for him to choose and hence which goods and services he actually purchases.

In other words, in this model, one of two factors can explain why two individuals may face two different sets of characteristics before the question of taste arises. The first such factor is real income: assuming prices are held constant, a lower income reduces what can be purchased and thus reduces the characteristics that can be produced. The second is inability: higher inability alters the household production process and thus reduces the characteristics that can be produced with any set of purchased goods and services. Either lower income or greater inability reduces the final level of utility.

Using this approach, an individual's needs can now be defined in two related ways. In terms of commodities purchased in the market, the consumer needs those goods and services that make up the least-cost bundle necessary to produce those characteristics associated with some minimum standard of living. In terms of money, he needs the amount that allows him to buy that least-cost bundle.

Lancaster's concepts also permit us to express the difference between variations in tastes and variations in needs. Two consumers have different tastes if they place different valuations on a characteristic that both can produce. For example, both may be able to purchase cars and drive them, but one may have no desire to do so. On the other hand, one has greater needs if inability reduces his capacity to produce, from a given set of inputs, any characteristic that is part of the set required for whatever level of well-being society has set as a minimum. For example, that minimum generally includes some form of transportation so the individual can shop for dinner, visit the doctor, see friends, have access to entertainment, and so on; a physically disabled person may have to spend far more than an average person to achieve such mobility. Similarly, that minimum utility probably includes being able to provide care for one's children; the parent of a handicapped child may require far more inputs than do other parents to do this.

Clearly, then, differences in ability affect the individual's utility, but we can safely call differences in tastes insignificant. So long as two consumers can produce the same sets of characteristics, then, so long as both are judged competent, public policy is indifferent to the choices each makes. If one prefers more fancy suppers and another more luxury transportation, we cannot say that either is better off.[9]

---

9 Stigler and Becker (1977, 77) go so far as to suggest that individuals may have quite similar tastes but differing endowments of various factors that enable them to produce commodities for consumption.

A new theory of in-kind transfers 33

The Lancasterian approach resolves the issue of needs and tastes theoretically, but how do we make the separation in practice? Sometimes the difference seems obvious. For example, we observe that chronically ill persons consume more medical care than average, but we also observe that some individuals consume more meals in French restaurants. The first action, we say, obviously indicates need, the second taste. In other words, being chronically ill reduces one's utility relative to others with the same income, while liking French food does not. In stating that the chronically ill person needs medical care while the gourmet does not need French food, we are arguing that medical care is part of the least-cost bundle required to maintain a minimum standard of living while French food is not.

Not all cases are so clear cut, however, and most are impossible to prove objectively because setting a minimum standard of living is itself an imprecise decision. Thus, ethical judgements are implicit in any statements about need and inability. However, the fact that these judgements are hard to justify quantitatively does not mean that public officials must make them arbitrarily. Lancaster suggested that the production of characteristics through consumption activities may be objective (that is, known by most consumers) (1966, 134). In that case, voters may agree which circumstances make household production more difficult (increase the inputs required to produce certain characteristics) and which do not. For example, they are likely to agree that illness, mental disability, and old age make production more difficult, while a desire for French food does not.

Another way to approach this question is by asking voters which conditions they would be willing to purchase insurance against, if such insurance were possible.[10] One would probably pay to insure against physical disability, lack of care in childhood, and retardation, but not against a taste for fine, tailored clothing.

With either approach, defining inability is no more arbitrary than defining a poverty line. Each requires a moral judgement about what minimum standards of well-being are to be guaranteed by social insurance.

The concepts of needs and inability are somewhat revolutionary in economic theory, but are quite similar to ideas familiar in other branches of the field. Development economists refer to 'basic needs' — the minimum requirements for achieving an acceptable standard of living — and they define these requirements in terms of goods and services, not income (see, for example, Streeten and Burki

---

10 Since many social problems are not insurable (private insurance is only practical if the individual can purchase it before the problem occurs, and many problems occur at birth or in adolescence), this may require a Rawlsian approach: asking voters to decide this in a mythical state in which none knows the condition of his life.

1978). It is not a large step to considering that individuals or families may differ in their basic needs, depending upon their inability.

Tax economists have long confronted the issue of different degrees of inability. In designing tax systems, they see that horizontal equity requires more than simply treating as equals all those with equal gross incomes. For example, both the Canadian and the U.S. tax systems recognize that above-average medical expenses represent need and should be subsidized in kind by allowing deductability. As one expert explained: 'The attitude seems to be that a person has little control over the amount of his medical expenses and that these expenses are unforseeable and sometimes catastrophically large. Above a certain normal level, medical expenses are regarded as a reduction of an individual's freely disposable income and hence a reduction in his ability to pay taxes relative to others with the same income' (Goode 1964, 166). This justification seems equivalent to the household production approach suggested above.

To summarize the argument so far, needs (as opposed to tastes) differ among individuals because abilities differ. Inability may be defined as any personal situation the consumer faces that makes him require higher-than-average inputs to produce a given set of characteristics and hence achieve a given minimum of well-being. When inability rises significantly above the norm, redistribution of income may not achieve equality of utility. To redistribute utility (if such a concept is meaningful), it may even be necessary to provide transfers to people whose incomes are above the average. For example, even if a profoundly disabled person has a fair-size income, he may require assistance to maintain an existence above poverty level. So may a family with a retarded child.

The crucial question is how much input an individual or family requires to achieve at least as much well-being (utility) as society has set as a minimum. When inability is great, the least-cost bundle needed for minimum utility may be very large and, therefore, very costly.

MEASURING INABILITY: THE COST OF INFORMATION

Of course, even great inability does not in itself justify in-kind programs. In theory, one can just alter the calculation of cash transfers so as to take inability into account. In practice, the efficiency of doing so depends on the cost of measuring the inability.

Altering cash transfers to compensate for inability is quite practical if the inability is easily (and hence cheaply) measured. For example, an increase in family size decreases the household's ability to achieve any given standard of living; family size should be easy to measure,[11] so it is relatively simple to build allowances for it into the computation of taxes or payment. This is done in both Canadian and U.S. income taxation (through exemptions for dependents) and in many general welfare programs. Age and certain kinds of physical disability are also easy to ascertain, and current tax law allows the old and some disabled people special, flat deductions.

Unfortunately, many kinds of inability are more difficult (and hence more expensive) to measure, especially when the information is to be used to adjust cash transfers or taxes. The individual being assessed generally has the best information about his level of inability (and hence his need), but he also has an incentive to exaggerate it in order to increase his cash transfer or reduce his taxes. Thus, in the absence of objective criteria of need, simply adjusting the cash transfer to allow for inability is not practical; if attempted, it is almost certain to be expensive and inefficient.[12]

Fortunately, the solution to the dilemma lies in the nature of inability. It usually stems from a specific problem or problems that cause the needy individual to require specific goods and services as remedies.[13] Hence, the kind and degree of inability may frequently be inferred from the individual's consumption of specific commodities. For example, an ill person consumes medical services, an incapacitated older person consumes care in a nursing home or by visiting nurses and homemakers, a physically disabled person consumes wheelchairs and special transportation services.

In cases such as these, where it is very difficult (and thus expensive) to identify the needy for special cash transfers, it may be less expensive to subsidize the particular good or service required by the individual or group in question. In a way, the subsidy allows the needy to self-select (generally an efficient process) because it is automatically of particular benefit to those who consume a large amount of the good.

Examples of several programs may illustrate these points. Consider first a health insurance program such as Ontario's. Suppose that an individual severely

11 Even family size is not always easy to measure. American welfare programs that provided assistance only to single-parent families encountered much difficulty (and expense) in determining when a father had genuinely deserted his family and when he was only temporarily absent in order to allow his family to qualify for welfare.
12 Remember, these criteria cannot depend on information about the goods and services purchased by the individual, since a cash transfer dependent upon consumption amounts to an in-kind subsidy. For example, adjusting taxable income (and hence taxes) to allow for day-care expenses is a form of subsidizing the purchase of day care.
13 A generalized inability – one that results in an individual's needing more than average of all goods and services – is theoretically possible, but it is more usefully viewed as a case of incompetence or a need for information (requiring counselling and education).

injures his knee. He receives, in kind, the medical care necessary to restore him to full health. In theory, of course, it would be more efficient to give him the cash equivalent of his medical care. Then he might choose to purchase the same level of care (and be equally well off), but he might prefer to purchase somewhat less care, leaving him with a slight limp and enough money to winter in Miami and be better off from his point of view.[14] But determining *in advance* the cash equivalent of medical care is an expensive procedure. The diagnostic procedures necessary to do so are part of the medical care itself and so represent a deadweight loss if the recipient then chooses to go to Miami. Also, some of the costs do not become clear until treatment is underway. Furthermore, if cash equivalents are handed out for medical care, significant resources have to be expended to prevent fraud, especially in the case of ailments that involve expensive treatment but are not immediately obvious (whiplash and other back injuries come to mind). Fraud is not a problem, however, when the prospective patient receives the medical care itself; there is an incentive to fake a knee injury for $4000 in cash but not for $4000 worth of treatment, including a knee operation.

Now consider rehabilitation programs for the disabled. Again, in theory it would be more efficient to give the recipient the cash equivalent of the services (counselling, education, and so on) he needs. But determining exactly which of those services are required is an expensive proposition and a complete waste of taxpayers' dollars if they are not then used. Moreover, part of the process of rehabilitation is periodic reassessment of exactly what services will benefit the recipient at particular points in the procedure.

Finally, consider visiting nurses and homemakers. Again, the cash equivalent of the required service could be given, but need is difficult to assess completely in advance. The present program allows modification of the services provided if the individual's need is not what was originally assessed. (For example, the frequency of visits can be increased if the recipient still cannot cope or if his circumstances change.)

Notice, however, that these examples compared pure in-kind transfers (those with no user charges) with equivalent cash transfers. Some middle ground (user charges below full cost) is possible and in most cases optimal. The reason is the same as the reason for the general inherent inefficiency of subsidies: the fact that a subsidy is so frequently a temptation to overconsumption.

---

14 The donor preference explanation of current policy has been to suggest that we (society, taxpayers) do not like people to limp around when they could be whole. In other words, the recipient's health, but not his Miami vacation, are in our utility functions. The theory of inability suggests a different justification for the same in-kind program.

This temptation varies primarily with the kind of good or service being subsidized. Consider the previous examples. Individuals without high inability and need do not have much use for knee operations or disability rehabilitation; consequently, the elasticity of demand for them is low. Individuals with much less need may, however, use visiting homemakers or other kinds of medical care. Although they may use smaller quantities, the elasticity of demand is fairly high.

In general, when the commodity is consumed only (or principally) by persons with inability, overuse is unlikely and high subsidies look attractive. Overuse is considerably more of a problem if the subsidized good or service is normally consumed, albeit in lesser quantities, by those who are not needy or only somewhat needy. Here low subsidies (higher user charges) can act as a deterrent. (The issue of overuse and inability is examined mathematically in Appendix B. The optimal setting of the subsidy rate, as dependent on the elasticity of demand and other factors, appears in the model and the computer simulations of Appendices C, D, and F.)

One further point must be made: fears of overuse and use by the nonneedy can be exaggerated when considering subsidies. In fact, in-kind programs can sometimes prevent transfers going to those who do not need them. The notion of inability, as it has been defined here, almost assumes that changes in price do not have much effect on the quantity of the service clients demand (that is, a low price elasticity of demand). Programs that assess and meet needs are inefficient only when the recipient, given the cash equivalent, would not choose to purchase quite so much of the commodity in question; when need is correctly assessed, a shift to cash transfers is unlikely to change consumption significantly. Those consumers for whom cash transfers are markedly more efficient may well be the very individuals who do not require assistance and who can best be filtered out by an in-kind program. For example, the man with the knee injury who chooses to use his cash transfer to go to Miami gains utility but reveals that his need was not as great as was estimated (either by mistake or by fraud). An in-kind program would likely filter him out.

A SUMMARY OF THE THEORY OF INABILITY

To summarize the argument: when individuals derive the same level of utility or well-being from a given level of income, a minimum level of well-being can be expressed in terms of money or a guaranteed annual income. In the absence of problems of externalities or incompetence, cash transfers can then provide what is necessary for clients to escape poverty.

All individuals do not, however, derive the same utility from a given level of income. Inability may affect utility so significantly that two poor individuals (or families) with the same income 'need' different levels of income to escape poverty. In these cases, cash transfers are still superior if they can easily be adjusted to compensate for these differences. But in many cases, it is not easy or inexpensive to acquire objective information about the true poverty line — that is, about the amount of extra income necessary to achieve the minimum level of utility for a particular recipient. This is especially true because the individual with the best information about that poverty line, the recipient himself, has every incentive to exaggerate his needs and inflate his cash transfer. Cash-transfer programs that attempt to differentiate thus are likely to end up redistributing too much money to the wrong people, while cash transfers that do not differentiate may leave those whose needs are great enough income to escape poverty.

In-kind subsidies can thus be justified as an efficient way to redistribute income if two conditions are present: 1) if inability is an important consideration in determining an individual's utility (given his income); *and* 2) if variations in inability cannot be easily measured for compensating cash transfers. When inability is present in individuals who are not poor, horizontal equity may justify subsidies for social services, just as it does in taxation. When in-kind subsidies are employed, however, some user charges may be appropriate to discourage overuse.

The algebraic model for this theory of inability, as applied to in-kind and cash transfers, is presented in Appendix C. It shows once again the greater efficiency of cash transfers in many circumstances — re-emphasizing the desirability of some form of negative income tax as the basis of antipoverty strategy — but demonstrates the superiority of goods-specific subsidies when the two conditions listed above are present. An algebraic solution for the optimal amount of subsidy shows it exists, rising with larger amounts of inability (as reflected in the marginal utility of income) *and* falling with greater elasticity of demand for the particular commodity.

Computer simulations, presented in Appendix D, showed the same thing: when the presence of hard-to-measure inability has a significant effect on utility and when the elasticity of substitution is not large, in-kind programs are efficient. Moreover, the simulations included a function resembling a negative income tax (or guaranteed annual income). They showed that even with such a tax in its optimal design, only in-kind programs can compensate for significant inability and maximize social welfare.

IN-KIND BENEFITS IN THE PRIVATE INSURANCE MARKET

Theories are the basis of the economist's work, but it is always wise to check them against the real world. One method of examining public programs is by comparing them to some private-sector equivalent whose economic workings are well understood. Since inability lowers well-being, government programs that assist the needy may be seen as compulsory social insurance against the occurrence of inability, and their operation can, in some ways, be compared to the operation of private insurance companies.[15]

Private insurance markets function because information is available. Detailed, relatively accurate statistics exist in most cases, showing the odds of a particular incident occurring (for example, of a man of a given age and state of health dying, a house in a given neighbourhood burning down, a person who regularly

15 Viewing social service programs as insurance raises the question of why the government makes coverage mandatory by having all taxpayers support the programs (in effect, pay the premiums) and all residents be eligible for this benefit. One reason is that the private sector may not offer suitable policies. The market depends on information about the client's risk. If companies cannot gauge risk and set premiums accordingly, adverse selection may occur: the insurers may be swamped by high-risk clients who drive the premium beyond the point at which a sufficient number of low-risk clients are willing to pay it; the risk pool is then destroyed, and companies must then stop offering the coverage or be driven out of business. (See Akerlof [1971] for a discussion of how inadequate information about quality can destroy markets, and Rothschild and Stiglitz [1975] for a more general discussion of information and insurance.)

Another point is even more relevant to the social services. Private insurance markets do not exist for events that take place before insurance can be purchased. Since the risk cannot be pooled, a person who is retarded or blind or deaf at birth is in no position to purchase insurance against his inability. This argument may hold for less extreme cases. For example, because of differences in makeup, individuals of the same age may face different risks of illness and hence different health insurance premiums in private markets with perfect information. By forcing everyone into the same risk pool, public health insurance implicitly transfers income to those at higher risk. (This situation fits into the theory of inability. Those at higher risk have more inability; full medical insurance coverage is part of their set of needs, and they have to pay more than average for it in the private insurance market.)

Private insurance markets are also useless when consumers are not aware of the risks facing them. For example, few young people realize the risks of old age. Even fewer newlyweds are likely to feel the need to insure against marital break-up and single parenthood. In both cases, by the time the risk becomes apparent, adverse selection almost ensures that private policies are unavailable. Again, a benevolent society provides benefits as if from insurance.

Musgrave (1968) offered another justification for compulsory insurance. Humanitarianism may lead society to intervene whenever income (or welfare) falls below a minimum level, even in situations where private insurance exists. For example, private companies offer disability insurance, but Ontario, like many jurisdictions, operates a vocational rehabilitation program for the seriously disabled. Yet the very guarantee of government help in the face of extreme disability may lead an imprudent individual to underinsure in the private market. To protect itself, society forces everyone, including the imprudent to contribute to public insurance against these catastrophes.

drives to work becoming involved in an accident). In writing policies, insurance companies use these statistics plus objective information that is either inexpensive to obtain (the client's date of birth, place of residence, and so on) or verifiable by some process that the client pays for (say, an appraiser's valuation or a laboratory's rating of a protective device). Then they can assign would-be clients to risk pools and set premiums accordingly.

Should the insured-against event occur, private insurance companies may find it most economical to pay benefits in cash. Again, the rationale is the availability of inexpensive, verifiable information. It is fairly easy to ascertain that a policyholder has died or that a building of stated value has burned down.

In many other cases, however, private insurance companies award various sorts of in-kind benefits. Private health insurance policies generally provide not a lump-sum settlement for each illness but reimbursement for the expenses incurred in obtaining treatment for that illness. Put in the terminology of this book, the beneficiaries receive not cash but a full or partial subsidy towards the purchase of those services necessary to restore good health and thus to compensate for an increase in need. Automobile insurance policies do exactly the same thing by paying for the repairs necessary to restore a damaged car to its previous state. Moreover, if a client becomes involved in a lawsuit, the insurance company generally assumes the job of protecting him in court and arranging any settlement. (The same provisions usually exist in other kinds of liability insurance.) And in homeowners', tenants', and movers' insurance policies, the insurer generally retains the option of repairing or replacing the damaged, destroyed, or stolen property, either directly or as reimbursement for actual expenses.

All these policies provide benefits in kind because the insurance company frequently has less information about the real value of the loss than does the customer. If benefits were provided in cash, recipients would have an incentive to overstate the amount of any loss and no incentive to minimize the odds of the loss occurring. These incentive problems fall under the category of what is often called moral hazard.

In the case of health insurance, for example, it is difficult (that is, expensive) for the insurer to assess the cost of treating an illness or injury before that treatment takes place. On the other hand, medical care, beyond that required to restore health, is of limited value to the recipient, so an in-kind payment decreases the patient's incentive to overstate his need.[16] Furthermore, if insurers

---

16 On the other hand, the superiority of in-kind payments for medical care is subverted if physicians respond to them by inducing patients to overuse medical services (since it is doctors rather than patients who decide how much care is required). Furthermore, some kinds of medical care (for example, face-lifts) *are* likely to be overused if the price of the service or the premium falls; for this reason, both public and private insurance programs generally handle them quite differently from other kinds of medical care.

provided a flat, lump-sum benefit for each category of illness or accident, clients would have to overinsure to ensure adequate coverage since the costs of care for medical problems in each category might vary significantly as treatment progressed.[17]

Liability insurance provides legal assistance and covers actual damages for similar reasons; moreover, the insurance company can effectively minimize the average cost of settlements by employing its own lawyers. If the company simply covered any loss, clients would have little incentive to minimize costs and the risk of fraud would increase. When writing property insurance, companies retain the right to repair the damaged goods because that is frequently the most effective way to secure information about the magnitude of the loss.

Since private insurance markets employ payments in kind, it is hardly surprising that social insurance programs do much the same thing. Whether insurance programs are private or public, they face similar information problems and use similar methods in dealing with them.

The theory of inability justifies in-kind payments as an effective way of meeting needs when information is inadequate. That is precisely the moral-hazard argument insurance companies use to explain the payment of benefits in kind. In fact, an empirical test of the theory of inability is the fact that private insurance companies make in-kind payments. Since they can hardly be motivated by paternalism or externalities (either conventional or donor preferences), we know they choose in-kind payments only when such payments meet their policy-holders' claims at the lowest possible cost. In other words, private health insurance pays for medical care in kind not because insurance executives prefer that a man with a broken knee receive medical care rather than limp around Miami Beach, but because the in-kind payment results in the most attractive policies. Because of moral hazard, cash settlements would cost companies too much and hence drive them out of a competitive market.

By the same token, the social services can sometimes meet the needs of recipients at least cost to the taxpayers by providing subsidized programs. In these cases, as in certain kinds of insurance coverage, the lack of inexpensive, objective information makes the in-kind benefit superior to cash payment.

IN-KIND TRANSFERS AND NEGATIVE INCOME TAXES

The theory of inability in no way negates the traditional economic preference for cash transfers. Rather, it expands the simple either/or argument and reaches the following conclusion: a comprehensive cash transfer system (some form of

---

17 For a fuller discussion of medical care, insurance, and overuse, see Barer, Evans, and Stoddard (1979).

negative income tax) must be a central part of any antipoverty strategy; nevertheless, the optimal feasible system still involves a significant number of in-kind programs that address a variety of specific needs.

The two parts of the conclusion are equally important. The first— that income redistribution is an essential part of any scheme to fight poverty — is quite clear to most economists. The poor require food, housing, clothing, and so on. Introducing the concept of need does not affect the superiority of using a cash transfer to provide these basics. The theory of inability identified two requirements for preferring an in-kind subsidy: that the elasticity of demand for the commodity be small and that variation in need be difficult to measure cheaply. Neither situation exists for the basics of food, clothing, housing, and so on. The poor, like everyone else, want more of these commodities than they actually need to achieve a minimum standard of living. The elasticity of demand for these items is high, and providing them in kind is likely to induce overconsumption. Moreover, variations in actual needs for these commodities are strongly linked to family size, an easily measured variable. Therefore, cash transfers dominate in-kind transfers in the provision of basics.

To put it another way, a negative income tax must be the foundation of alleviating poverty. Even when a client has special needs best met through in-kind transfer, if he is capable of making competent economic decisions, his *basic* needs must still be addressed through a cash-transfer system.[18]

The view of subsidy programs as backing up a welfare program based on adequate cash transfers is scarcely original. For example, Bird recently argued that 'society would be much better served by (a) a more adequate income security plan *and* (b) more rational uses of pricing in other public services ... Income redistribution and benefits financing [subsidized programs with user charges] are necessary complements, not substitutes as the naive might think. Each one alone has less justification than the two together' (Bird 1976, 159).[19]

The need for basing antipoverty strategy on cash transfers is quite clear to many noneconomists working in the field. For example, a federal-provincial working party on social service funding reported:

---

18 In the simulations developed in Appendix D, the presence of significant immeasurable inability is what raises the value of the variable NEED. When NEED is low, the value of the optimal subsidy s is low, and utility is redistributed mainly through the cash-transfer system. Even when NEED is large, significant cash transfers are still a fundamental part of the optimal redistributive system.
19 Bird's book is a persuasive case for user charges and should be compulsory reading for anyone making policy in this area.

To a major extent, the success of social services is highly dependent on the users' basic financial needs being met. While certain services provide assistance that can be measured in dollar values, it is important to note that no amount of social services can ever make up for serious income deficiencies. By the same token, social services should never be viewed as a substitute for the assurance of an adequate income. To do so is to subvert the objectives of social services and to jeopardize considerably their potential success in dealing with human problems. (Working Party on Social Services 1974, 22)

The report's insistence on a two-pronged system is wise. Although an adequate cash-transfer system is badly needed, it is possible for economists to overestimate the simplifications in the welfare system its introduction would occasion. For example, Milton Friedman, in proposing a negative income tax to alleviate poverty, argued: 'The advantages of this arrangement are clear. It is directed specifically at the problem of poverty. It gives help in the form most useful to the individual, namely, cash. It is general and could be substituted for the host of special measures now in effect ... if enacted as a substitute for the same end, the total administrative burden would surely be reduced' (Friedman 1962, 192-3).

While it is certainly true that one would expect most food and housing programs to disappear under a negative income tax, many other social programs would, in fact, continue, and others might be introduced. This is the second part of the conclusion – that the optimal feasible system must involve a significant number of in-kind programs – and it represents the main contribution of this chapter.

Again, the theory of inability does not contradict traditional theory. When consumers are incompetent or ill-informed, when the government wishes to redistribute within the family, when externalities exist, subsidies may be more desirable than cash transfers for reasons that are not directly related to inability as defined in this chapter. But these traditional justifications have never been able to account for very many programs in the social services. The new concept – inability – justifies considerably more.

When a certain ability varies so significantly among consumers that it has an important influence on utility and hence on who is or is not poor, any scheme purporting to maximize social welfare must address inability. If the particular inability is easy to measure, it can be compensated by varying the cash transfer. Often, however, there is no inexpensive and reliable way to judge a client's need. In that case, it is likely to be more efficient to subsidize the purchase of whatever goods and services he requires to meet that particular need. The in-kind transfer is superior to cash here because it reduces the client's incentive to exaggerate his inability (that is, to purchase more of the commodity than he would if it were unsubsidized). This reduction occurs when the value of additional units of the commodity falls off rapidly once clients' needs have been met. If this does not occur, the elasticity of demand is large and in-kind subsidies are less attractive, although they may be necessary if inability is great and very difficult to measure.

Many social services meet specific but difficult-to-measure needs. Even if we had an optimal cash transfer system providing the poor with basics, in-kind programs would still have a role wherever there is significant, immeasurable inability and need.[20]

CONCLUDING REMARKS

The theory of inability has been repeated too often in this chapter to require any but the briefest concluding summary. Inability may be defined as any endowment or situation that causes an individual to require higher-than-average inputs to produce the characteristics society has decided are part of achieving some minimum level of well-being. When inability makes individuals significantly worse off than those who lack it and when its magnitude is not easily (cheaply) identifiable, countering it with in-kind transfers is efficient (see Appendix C).

Thus, inability can be added to incompetence and conventional externalities as a legitimate exception to the general superiority of cash transfers. Like these traditional exceptions, inability provides a defensible justification for subsidized social services designed to counter it. Unlike these other instances, it is applicable to a fairly large number of circumstances encountered by social planners. It is by no means, however, a justification for any in-kind program that strikes the policy-maker's fancy; cash transfers remain clearly superior for many circumstances, including the provision of basics such as food and housing. Neither is it always a justification for full subsidy; the calculations in Appendices C and D

---

20 See equation (C.21). Equation (C.22) argues that in-kind transfers should occur as long as there is a group of needy individuals who use a particular commodity (the need-good X) and whose general level of well-being is lower than that of the average welfare recipient.

The simulations of Appendix D show that as the degree of immeasurable inability rises, the cash-transfer system alone becomes increasingly inadequate, and the gains from an in-kind subsidy become increasingly important in maximizing social welfare. For example, when inability is set at the highest value used in the program, increasing the cash transfer actually *reduces* the relative welfare of many consumers who have below-average utilities because they have higher-then-average incomes (see Table D.5). An in-kind transfer – in one case, equivalent to subsidizing over two-thirds of the cost of the needed commodity – is necessary to achieve the highest possible social welfare.

show it more often suggests partial subsidies (and hence the imposing of user charges). This is true mainly because the efficiency of countering inability with in-kind transfers decreases as the elasticity of demand for a commodity rises.

In use, the concept of inability solves or at least explains a number of problems in social service programs, as discussed in the following chapters. And when added to traditional justifications for in-kind transfers, it gives the economist a tool with which to differentiate between efficient and inefficient subsidies. Not least important is the fact that this theory is one that directly addresses the concerns of social policy-makers.

Thus, we have travelled full circle and arrived where we began: at the need to incorporate the world as perceived by social planners into an economic model of reality. The theory of inability described in this chapter (and modelled in Appendix C) seems to do this because it starts with the concepts of inability and need, concepts that are of obvious concern in the social services. It also meets the pragmatic test of making arguments parallel to those often heard from social planners. For example, the federal-provincial working party of 1974 developed a list of nine principles its members wanted to see applied to systems of user charges. At least five of them coincide with the theory of inability, although they are expressed in very different language. (For a complete list of these principles, see Appendix E.) Clearly, the theory relates to the concerns of both economists and social planners.

4
Some practical problems in in-kind programs

Once an economist has identified a particular sort of social service program as efficient, he cannot say his task is complete, any more than the planner can stop working once he has identified a social need and a way to meet it. In both cases, the professional must consider the program's design—exactly what goods it covers, how eligibility is determined, the rate of any user charge, and so on. Moreover, he must consider these things not only in relation to the program itself, but in the way they may affect general social goals (such as minimizing costs for the taxpayer and encouraging participation in the work force) and in the way they may interact with other social programs.

It is in these considerations that the designer is likely to encounter problems. Whether a program is a cash or an in-kind transfer, whether it is justified by inability or by older theories of incompetence and conventional externalities, it is almost bound to involve contradictions and competing goals. Some of these problems have solutions; others are inevitable, although their effects can often be mitigated. Economists and social planners alike must operate in an imperfect world, where success in one area risks unfavourable results in another and achieving almost anything involves compromise. We would do well to remember that the familiar word 'trade-off' is a synonym for 'compromise'.

This chapter is a compromise. Its confines are far too small to allow examination of every problem encountered in setting user charges for social services programs. It touches, therefore, only on those that seem especially common or important, with particular but not exclusive reference to goods-specific programs justified by the presence of inability, dealing successively with design techniques for targeting and other goals, with various incentive problems, and with the integration of programs.

The point is neither to argue that all subsidy programs currently operating in Ontario or other jurisdictions are perfectly designed nor to claim that they are

Some practical problems 47

all economic disasters. Rather, it is to suggest that in some cases 'obvious' inefficiencies are either unavoidable or not worth the trade-offs that would be necessary to correct them. In other cases, however, improvements are possible after consideration of a particular program's goals, of who qualifies for it under existing regulations, and of what its effects are on recipients and on society.

BALANCING COMPETING GOALS WITHIN A PROGRAM

All in-kind transfer programs, no matter what their economic justification, have the same general aim: providing a particular commodity to a specific target group. In an ideal world, each individual in that group would receive the commodity in the exact amount he or she needs, and this would be accomplished at the lowest possible cost to the taxpayer. In real life, both goals — getting benefits to the people who need them and achieving low cost (efficiency) — are often impossible to achieve completely. Moreover, they are likely to compete with each other.

In the case of subsidy programs justified by inability, this competition is based in large part on a paradox. The more precisely in-kind transfers can be targeted to the needy and the closer actual benefits come to the optimal subsidy, the more effective the transfer is.[1] But if precise targeting could be accomplished easily, the in-kind transfer would not be justified in the first place (because the needy target group could then be identified easily, making a cash transfer superior).

Nevertheless, despite the difficulties in identifying inability, the program designer must attempt to target for it. By definition, a subsidy justified as compensation for inability must reach those who most need it.[2] Although this statement seems obvious, a computer simulation was run to check it (see Appendix F). A prior set of simulations (those reported in Appendix D) had made a need-justified program available to all consumers; the results suggested that this wide availability diluted the subsidy's effectiveness and reduced its optimal size.

---

1 In terms of the model of Appendix C, efficiency and the size of the optimal subsidy increase directly with inability and inversely with the elasticity of demand (the responsiveness of demand to the reduction in price effected by the subsidy).
2 The kind of targeting being discussed must be differentiated from showcasing. A government designs a showcase program to deal only with those in extreme need and ignores all other potential recipients. The supply of the subsidized good and/or the number of recipients made eligible for subsidy is extremely limited. The intent is to generate political capital without spending very much (or, in fact, making much of a dent in the problem).

This time the simulation restricted the subsidy to recipients with significant inability.

Not surprisingly, this targeting improved total social welfare, redistributed utility away from individuals without inability towards those with high inability, and generally increased the optimal subsidy. However, it also had a perverse effect: it often gave greater welfare to individuals with great inability than it did to those with the same income but less inability.

This problem often occurs in programs because of what administrators call notches: points at which a slight increase in ability or in income results in a substantial reduction of benefits.[3] Another reason is the fuzziness of the boundaries between eligibility and ineligibility for a program or between one rate of subsidy and another.

These concerns are not merely theoretical. Administrators in many social services — day care and care for the elderly, to name but two — are often criticized because their programs seem arbitrary, if not outright unfair. Sometimes individuals who are living in very unfortunate circumstances are ineligible for targeted subsidies while others whose need is less obvious are eligible. Sometimes, too, program design seems to encourage use of the subsidized good by individuals who might be better served by a less costly alternative.

These problems are inherent in targeting in the absence of perfect information about the actual need of each recipient. As we saw in Chapter 3, the existence of moral hazard often makes it impossible to obtain accurate, objective information about clients' true need. Hence, it is impossible to determine exactly who requires how much of a given commodity. Various programming devices currently used in Ontario and other jurisdictions all improve targeting, hold down costs, or both, but none, alone or in combination, is able to ensure absolutely efficient allocation of benefits so as to exactly compensate for each client's need. If program design places great importance on reaching persons who have the greatest need, it may eliminate those with lesser (though still significant) need. If it stresses reaching everyone in need, costs skyrocket and/or the size of the subsidy decreases dramatically. And in any case, the difficulty in exactly assessing need causes inequities in any eligibility requirements.

Clearly, if the social services of Ontario (or anywhere else) existed in a world of perfect information, program designers would have an easy solution: define need precisely and arrange subsidies accordingly. Because this is impossible, they generally attempt two types of devices, often in combination. The first is to

---

3 Technically, a notch refers to a point in an income-tested program, but by extension we can also speak of need notches.

restrict the kinds of goods eligible for subsidy to those used primarily by people with great inability; the second is to restrict the classes of persons eligible for the subsidy to those with great need. Both types of restrictions tend to be arbitrary; in a perfect world, both would be inefficient. Their apparently haphazard results reflect the untidy, imperfect world faced by economists and social planners when they tackle the design of subsidy programs.[4]

Limits on the type of good subsidized
Perhaps the easiest, most effective way to target an in-kind transfer is to limit the kind of commodity eligible for subsidy in a way that makes it useful only to persons who have great inability. For example, persons in wheelchairs have a greater-than-average need for transportation services. (To use the theoretical terminology of Chapter 3, they require more inputs than do the less handicapped to produce the same level of the characteristic 'transportation'.) One could compensate for their inability by providing them with a general subsidy for all kinds of transportation, but such a program would be difficult (costly) to police and would still probably draw would-be recipients from outside the specific group of needy persons it was designed for. A more effective design is to provide this group with special transportation — wheelchairs and specially designed wheelchair vans. Although it is theoretically possible for an able person to take advantage of such a subsidized service, it is unlikely that anyone who does not need it would suffer its inconvenience or risk the disgrace of being found out. In any case, if the service is not highly subsidized, its price, even after subsidy, may not be attractive to someone not in special need.

Since the point of the subsidy is to compensate for inability, the user charge for this sort of limited-use commodity can often be set by benchmarking — providing the good or service at a charge equal to what a normal person would pay for the equivalent end product. Thus the cost of a benchmarked ride in a wheelchair van, including assistance into and out of the vehicle, can be set equal to the cost of a cab ride to the same destination.

Benchmarking is a particularly useful concept for setting user charges in situations where the process of providing the service includes assessing inability

---

4 Arbitrary results are not limited to in-kind programs but are also present in many current cash-transfer programs. For example, Ontario's Family Benefits program differentiates a 'disabled person' from one who is 'permanently unemployable' (according to the degree to which each is limited in normal activities). The financial implications of falling on one side of the line or the other are significant. Frequently those who are 'unfortunate' enough not to have quite enough disability to qualify end up far worse off financially than do those whose disability is somewhat higher.

and hence setting the future type and level of service. A user charge for medical care, for example, can be assessed per visit or per illness, independent of the level of treatment required. A flat charge for counselling can be levied without reference to the amount of service required, and a charge for a developmental child-care program can be independent of any particular special programs required by an individual child.[5]

Limits by rough tests for great inability
Limiting the subsidy to a commodity that is primarily useful only to the target group is a highly effective device, especially if the user charge can be benchmarked, but the technique presumes that such a commodity exists. Unfortunately this is often not the case. Many need-commodities are used by persons with and without inability or by persons with various degrees of inability. When this is the case, targeting becomes much more difficult — but also much more necessary if the program is to relieve significant need without prohibitive cost.

When the need-good is not amenable to limits, the most obvious method of targeting is to limit the recipients to persons who have great inability. Accurate tests for inability are, however, expensive and may not even be possible. As a compromise, some programs use very rough tests of inability. They are likely to identify extreme inability with fair accuracy, but they may be quite arbitrary when it comes to selecting recipients whose need is somewhat less although still significant.

Take, for example, the way in which the province of Ontario selects recipients for its limited number of subsidized day-care places. Institutional day care is a good desired by many families with many degrees of inability and need. Taxpayers are not willing to support enough subsidized places for all the needy families who desire them. Consequently, the program's designers have established a rough but inexpensive gauge of great need. The program gives first priority to children whose parents are unable to care for them because of physical or mental illness. The remaining subsidized spaces go to the children of working parents (provided they meet an income test), with preference given to single-parent families.

The aim is to target the spaces to families who need them the most — that is, to those parents who can most benefit from working, who most need help with

---

5 This, of course, is not to presume that a user charge is necessarily desirable for any of these programs. If it is unwise to discourage consumption because of externalities (say, in the case of counselling or education) or because of consumers' poor information (perhaps in the case of counselling or medical care), then no user charge should be levied.

Some practical problems 51

child rearing, and who have no access to cheaper, high-quality child care (such as a relative willing to care for the children). The last point is clearly impossible to prove for any given family. The other two are partly addressed by giving subsidies primarily to single-parent families. The rationale for the test is not that single parents do not enjoy their children or are incapable of raising them; rather, it is that single parents with low incomes are easily identifiable and are assumed to be more likely than many parents to have a difficult time with young children and to benefit from some support (day care) and encouragement to work. That the test misses some who could benefit from help – single parents with higher incomes or most two-parent families– is the unfortunate result of the impossibility of accurate targeting. If anyone were able to invent a more accurate, inexpensive way of assessing the need for day care, social service agencies would probably adopt it.

Limits on the amount of the commodity subsidized
Another limit often used for subsidized goods that appeal to a wide range of consumers is restricting the quantity of the commodity that a client may purchase and still remain eligible for the subsidy program. This device can serve two goals: it may prevent overconsumption by some clients and hence reduce inefficiency; it may also eliminate from the program consumers who are not poor by offering substantially less of the good than they would normally want to consume.

The goal of preventing overconsumption is connected with the elasticity of demand. As shown in Appendices B and C, the larger the elasticity of demand, the larger the loss of efficiency and the lower the optimal subsidy.[6] But if the consumer can be forced to consume less of the subsidized good than he might prefer, the subsidy may be efficient.

Clearly, setting a limit to prevent overuse of the subsidized commodity can be effective only if we can assume that most consumers eligible for the program have similar demands for the good. This assumption raises two technical problems. The first is that it requires that demand not vary greatly with income. If such variation exists, forcing all consumers to purchase the same amount of the good means that many end up consuming either more or less of it than is efficient.[7]

---

6 See equations (B.9), (C.22), and (C.30).
7 A computer simulation of a need-justified subsidy was run, using a simplication of the model in equation (C.31). It held labour (and income) fixed, so that consumers maximized $u_i = \left\{ a(X_i - n_i)^{-b} + (1-a) E_i^{-b} \right\}^{-d/b}$. The simulation showed that blanket limits on consumption were consistently inefficient, whatever the parameters. This result is not surprising since the income elasticity of the demand for X, given the CES

The second problem is that demand depends upon inability that varies significantly. (This is one of the initial conditions for justifying the in-kind subsidy in the first place.) Fixing the quantity of the good provided is likely, therefore, to supply too little of it to clients with the highest inability or too much to those with somewhat less inability.

Both problems can be dealt with. Even if demand varies with income, limits on the quantity subsidized can be useful if the program is limited to persons in a particular income bracket. The variation in inability is not serious if the amount of the commodity provided is adjusted to account for inability, as happens when part of the program is determining just how much of the service the consumer requires (as in, for example, health care, special education, vocational rehabilitation and visiting nurses and homemakers). In all these cases, however, some inequities may exist because even measurement by professionals may be somewhat arbitrary.

Limiting the quantity of a subsidized good can also meet the second goal (discouraging its use by persons who are not poor) if demand varies with income. However, this effect may not be compatible with the first goal (preventing overuse), which requires that such variation be small. And once again, if limits are placed on quantity, many of the poor who do receive the subsidy are likely to consume an inefficient amount of the commodity (either too much or too little to compensate for their inability). It would seem more efficient simply to disqualify everyone who has over a certain income. Sometimes, however, policymakers feel income tests are undesirable; in these cases, limits on quantity can make programs less desirable to those able to pay their own way and thus spare the taxpayers the cost of providing services to the well-to-do.

The problems of substitutes
As demonstrated in Chapter 3, low price elasticities of demand are necessary to justify significant in-kind subsidies. One condition for a low price elasticity is that no close, comparably priced substitutes be available. The subsidized commodity must be carefully defined to achieve this. One approach in program

---

function above, is approximately one (this is strictly true when $n = 0$). However, for many goods associated with inability, one might expect income elasticities to be somewhat less than one (if the good is indeed a necessity). Thus, effective prevention of overconsumption by comsumption limits requires both low income elasticities and high price elasticities of demand (since overconsumption is only a problem if the elasticity of demand is significant). In practice, these requirements severely restrict the number of programs to which effective limitation is applicable.

design, therefore, is to subsidize all close substitutes and to structure the subsidy so that it does not induce potential consumers to make an inefficient choice.

A simple example may clarify these concepts. Suppose that consumers consider goods A and B to be very close substitutes and hence simply purchase whichever is less expensive. If it costs $1500 to produce A and $3000 to produce B, consumers normally purchase A. Now suppose that the government decides to subsidize the purchase of B by 80 per cent (imposing a user charge of $600). Recipients switch from A to B, preferring to pay $600 rather than $1500. They feel that the subsidy saves them $900. The subsidy's actual cost to the government, however, is $2400. Unless consumers consider B (without a subsidy) to be worth $1500 more than A (in which case, the two are not close substitutes), they always value the subsidy at less than its cost to the government.

One obvious solution is for the government to subsidize A and B (and C and D, too, if they are also close substitutes). In some cases, however, policy dictates subsidizing only B. Perhaps the government regards it as superior to A and wishes consumers to purchase it.[8] However, unless B is actually worth at least $1500 more than A, the subsidy is inefficient.

Often the relative value of A and B depends on the inability of the consumer. We have already seen that one way to target an in-kind transfer to the needy is to subsidize only commodities useful to persons with a high level of inability. B may be very valuable (that is, worth more than $1500 more than A) to persons with high inability and much less valuable to those with low inability. If most individuals outside the target group perceive B as worth less than A by more than $900, they will not purchase it even with an 80 per cent subsidy, and the subsidy is efficient. (This is the situation described in the prior example of providing special transportation for the handicapped.)

The problem arises when inability is a continuum, so that some consumers prefer B to A but by less than $1500 or prefer A to B but by less than $900. With the subsidy, these consumers buy B, although purchasing A would be more efficient for society as a whole.

We have already seen that trying to provide a subsidized good only to persons who have great inability is bound to be somewhat clumsy; the program almost inevitably misses some consumers who are in need, while others with high inability may well end up better off than those with less inability and the same income. The inefficiency described here is the other side of the same coin.

---

8 Notice, however, that elements of paternalism may enter here, perhaps justifying an otherwise inefficient subsidy.

Consumers with relatively low inability do not value the subsidized commodity as much as those with high inability, but members of the former group may still purchase the commodity *because* it is subsidized, even though that purchase is inefficient.

An example can illustrate these points. Ontario provides subsidized care in homes for the aged; it is targeted at the elderly whose inability is so great that they cannot care for themselves. Some old people who have slightly less inability can manage to some degree by themselves; they eke out an existence in unfortunate circumstances but may not qualify for various other forms of assistance, even if their incomes are quite low. Their lesser inability results in their having lower well-being than the aged who qualify for institutional care. Other elderly persons in much the same situation, however, manage to qualify for subsidized homes and enter them, although less expensive kinds of assistance, if available, would allow them to live in the community at a lower cost to the taxpayer and in a manner they would probably prefer. They choose living in an institution, even though it means giving up the independence they probably value, because it is the subsidized (lowest cost) option available.[9] If subsidies were available for all kinds of care for the aged, this inefficiency would not occur. However, programming in this manner would lose the advantages of targeting the most available funds to those with the greatest inability.

Income tests

As we have seen, when the good to be subsidized is attractive to persons with various degrees of inability and cannot be limited in kind or quantity, it can sometimes be targeted by restricting the recipients. Rough tests (such as being a single parent or being unable to care for oneself) provide inexpensive if arbitrary sorting of potential recipients. Other kinds of tests are somewhat more expensive, and hence their use must be a trade-off for increased efficiency. Often, however, that increase is quite large, if the tests are properly designed.

One time-hallowed method of limiting recipients is to limit the subsidy to persons whose incomes are below a certain level. Generally, the program design has the user charge rise with income so as to reach full cost (zero subsidy) when income exceeds some amount. If variations in inability are not so important to utility distribution that they completely dominate variations in income (that is, if a high-income individual with a high level of inability is not reduced to

---

9 A parallel situation existed during the 1960s. At that time Ontario did not subsidize nursing homes (except for persons on welfare), but OHIP subsidized hospital care. Then hospital care looked more attractive to patients even though many of them could have been cared for in nursing homes at much lower cost.

Some practical problems 55

poverty), income tests can increase the optimal subsidy and indicate persons whose inability and general circumstances make them a target for redistribution.

It must be noted, however, that income-testing subsidy programs are significantly more effective when cash-transfer programs are also available to ensure that the in-kind programs are not used to compensate for inadequate incomes.

A simple example can illustrate this principle. Suppose that income is distributed so that the poorest individual in the economy has none; suppose, too, that inability is distributed randomly in the population and that it acts as a lump-sum tax, so that an individual with inability N and income I can be said to have an income-equivalent (utility) of $I - N$. Thus an individual with income 9000 and inability 4000 is as well off as someone with income 5000 and inability 0.

Assume that the largest value of N is 4000 and that the general aim of policy is to ensure that no one's income-equivalent is below 5000. One way to accomplish this is to design a negative income tax with a basic support level of 9000 (so as to reach the individual for whom N = 4000 and I = 0).[10] However, this cash-transfer system determines eligibility by income. It cannot earmark persons whose inability is high, so this scheme lacks horizontal equity; it treats differently the individual with I = 2000 and N = 0 and the individual with I = 6000 and N = 4000, although the two start with the same income-equivalent. Moreover, it is very expensive.

Another way to achieve the same goal is to design the negative income tax with a basic level of support of 5000 and supplement it with in-kind programs to reach the needy whom it leaves with income-equivalents below 5000 (in other words, to use income-tested programs directed only to those with inability). This twofold design is more equitable and less expensive than attempting to solve all problems with a negative income tax *or* with subsidy programs.

This fact was strikingly demonstrated by a computer simulation refining the one that restricted the subsidy to persons with significant inability (see Appendix F). This time the program limited subsidy recipients to persons whose wage rates were below a certain level. Although the particular test used (varying the subsidy according to wage rate, not earned income) was somewhat unrealistic (a point addressed in the appendix), the general result suggested that income-testing can raise social welfare, as well as allow larger subsidies. In other words, a subsidy program that has no income test is all too likely benefiting persons who have both high inability and high incomes. Assuming inability does not dominate

---

10 Here and elsewhere in this chapter, the term 'negative income tax' is used in the generic sense to include all guaranteed annual income programs, not just those that deliver benefits through the tax system.

income, these consumers have higher utilities (and hence lower marginal utilities of income) than others who do not have inability but have low incomes and so lose under a general goods-specific subsidy.[11] Targeting according to income raises the optimal subsidy and often the social benefits of the program.

Income-testing may, however, make individuals with both inability and low incomes better off than those with inability and relatively high incomes, especially if the subsidy falls off too quickly as income rises. One result then, of course, is a disincentive to earn income. The program designer can sometimes solve this problem by making the fall-off gradual. Often, however, he does better to consider how the subsidy can be integrated into the whole incentive structure of a negative income tax and how it interacts with the subsidy structures of other social service programs, subjects discussed later in this chapter.

Needs tests

Some social services assess user charges on the basis of needs tests rather than income tests. Needs tests take into consideration not only income but what the client spends on goods other than the one being subsidized (in other words, they adjust income for actual expenses).[12] The calculation of the user charge for Ontario's subsidized day-care program, for example, includes the recipient family's housing costs (rent or mortgage payments), the cost of special medicines it requires, and payments it must make on any loans; these expenditures reduce the user charge dollar for dollar (up to a maximum in the case of rent).

The purpose of the needs test is to permit different treatment of clients who are in different situations, to take into account the extraordinary expenses some face. Understanding that differences in income are not the only consideration in assessing need, program designers work on the assumption that an individual or family with larger-than-average expenses in certain key areas has less available income to spend on the commodity being needs-tested. Thus, needs tests are in the spirit of the theory of inability.

The major difficulty with needs-testing is that it assumes that increases in expenditures in a number of key areas reflect greater need. Here again is a moral-hazard problem: recipients may have an incentive to inflate their purchases in these areas so as to qualify for increased subsidies under the needs test. The designer's problem then is to separate increases in expenditures that are

---

11 In the model in Appendix C, the lack of an income test raises the utilities of those eligible for in-kind transfers relative to the utilities of other welfare recipients and other taxpayers.
12 Needs tests also frequently use wealth or asset tests; they disqualify for subsidy an individual who has liquid (and sometimes illiquid) assets of more than a certain amount. Income tests generally consider only income flows, though this need not be the case.

caused by accidents or bad luck from those arising from conscious attempts to exploit the testing method.

In some areas, this problem is unimportant. In theory, clients might rent better accommodations (up to the low maximum in the Ontario needs test) or take vacations so as to accumulate consumer debt and thus reduce their need-tested user charges, but no evidence exists to suggest that they act in this manner. In any case, case workers can presumably prevent abuses after an individual or family is in the program.

A more serious issue arises in the Ontario needs test's treatment of mortgage payments. Here no maximums apply and additional expenses may well result in higher quality.[13] Moreover, renters and buyers receive unequal treatment. In a period of high inflation, high nominal mortgage rates include in them a significant amount of real amortization of outstanding debt, so the mortgagee may build up significant equity. Subsidizing mortgage payments may thus be unfair to the renter who cannot enjoy the same increase in his assets.[14]

The concern about mortgage debt can be extended to consumer debt in general. Including debt repayments in the needs test may be inequitable if the client incurred the debt by purchasing consumer durables that now provide a stream of services (a stream not available to the family without debts and without those durables). On the other hand, his debt may reflect past expenditures on nondurables, in which case there is no offsetting stream of benefits. Since distinguishing these two cases is difficult (again, moral hazard arises), the decision to include debt repayments in the needs test may be appropriate.

Generally, caseworkers prefer needs-testing to income-testing, in part because the former gives workers more discretion, in part because the latter is usually harsher and results in the average family's paying a higher user charge than it does under a needs test. On the other hand, since needs-testing is more complicated than income-testing and hence more expensive, it should be employed only where the ability to adjust for need is clearly desirable.

Restricting programs: an overview
In summary, the redistributional power of a need-justified in-kind transfer is greatly enhanced (and the argument for the subsidy strengthened) if the subsidy

---

13 On the other hand, the rise in housing prices over the last ten years leads one to suspect that the size of mortgage payments may be influenced more by when the house was purchased than by its quality. If that is true, allowing mortgage payments as an expense corrects for inequities among homeowners.
14 This concern may become more important if the needs test for certain commodities (day care, for example) is liberalized to extend the subsidy to wealthier users who are more likely to own homes.

can be limited to persons who have the greatest inability and/or those who have the lowest incomes (in other words, to those with higher marginal utilities of income). Targeting the program to these individuals increases the optimal subsidy. Moreover, on a practical level, the easiest way to limit a program's costs is to reduce the number of people eligible for the subsidy and increase the number paying full cost or close to full cost for the commodity.

Conceptually, it is relatively easy to restrict a subsidy to persons with low incomes; restricting it to those with the greatest inability is harder. The problem is that inability is often not identifiable at low cost. When it is, cash transfers and not subsidies are called for. Since low income, easy-to-identify inability, and hard-to-identify inability can all contribute to need, and since the first two are best countered by cash transfers, antipoverty strategy calls for a combination of some form of negative income tax and income-tested subsidy programs.

In the real world, even income is not really easy (or inexpensive) to measure, especially when it changes over time as wages change and jobs are obtained and lost.[15] But at least adjusting for income allows the gradual removal of the subsidy (raising of user charges) as income rises (unless this is undesirable for some other reason, such as the presence of externalities or incompetence because of consumers' poor information).

Since assessing inability is far more difficult than assessing income, programs that depend on the former are likely to result in the drawing of arbitrary boundaries. One of the most efficient methods is that of limiting the subsidy to goods primarily used by persons with high levels of inability; even this technique can produce arbitrary and sometimes inefficient results at the margins. Moreover, some need-goods cannot be so closely defined. Reducing the subsidy gradually as need declines is desirable but often impractical to do exactly; again the result is often notches. Subsidizing close substitutes may remove or lessen the notches; it also improves efficiency but loses the advantages of targeting for the most serious inability.

Restricting subsidies to persons with great inability and/or low income is consistent with the view of social service programs as compulsory insurance expressed in Chapter 3. The purpose of insurance is to protect the individual against events that would cause his utility to fall below some minimum set by society. Limiting the programs to individuals whose inability is significant is consistent with the insurance principle of protecting only against abnormal losses. (The assumption is that most people prefer to self-insure against minor risks—hence the deductible provisions common in many insurance policies.)

---

15 In theory, of course, all subsidies could be handled through income tax credits and deductions, but further complications of the tax form are also not free.

From an insurance viewpoint, limiting programs by income is more open to question, since even the affluent want insurance protection against very large losses. Two considerations, however, may make income-testing efficient. The first is that the absolute magnitude of what is considered a significant loss rises as income rises. An individual with a relatively high income can, in effect, self-insure against losses that might be disasterous for a poorer person.

The second consideration is somewhat broader: social insurance is frequently meant to protect not so much against specific events but against any combination of circumstances that might cause utility to fall below some minimum. A wealthy person can suffer considerable inability before requiring assistance to avoid falling below some minimum level of well-being.

This last point can be generalized. When a public program is meant to replace private insurance that the wealthy would purchase anyway (for example, health insurance or disability insurance), income-testing the benefits is not appropriate. But when a public program is part of an overall scheme of social insurance against poverty, income-testing may be appropriate. It should be noted, however, that even if a subsidy is properly income-tested, it may not be appropriate to eliminate it entirely for persons with high incomes. Here the principle of horizontal equity suggests that some allowance be made for inability, perhaps through some form of deductibility.

PROBLEMS IN MAINTAINING INCENTIVES

When an economist considers program design, he cannot restrict himself to methods of getting benefits to the people who need them most. Maintaining efficiency also means providing benefits at the least possible cost to the taxpayer. Neither can the efficiency of a single program be considered in a vacuum. In theory and in practice, policy-makers, program designers, and economists must examine a program's effects on other programs' benefits and efficiencies and the way the program fits into the overall antipoverty or social welfare effort — all points that have been touched on already in this book and that will recur. Furthermore, because the entire economy is interconnected, consideration must be given to the program's effects on the labour force and hence on tax revenues, as well as on savings.

The length of this book precludes a complete examination of these areas, but it is useful to look at some of them. Many of the problems that arise in these areas can be loosely grouped as problems of incentive — a term economists use in its precise, dictionary definition: something outside an individual that prompts him to act in a particular way. The particular ways in which economists want individuals to act are those that contribute to overall efficiency and hence the general welfare. Whatever their personal codes, as economists they want people to enter the work force, to refrain from taking benefits they do not truly need, and so on, not for moral reasons or a belief in the work ethic but because these actions increase overall efficiency. Similarly, they know that incentive problems exist in social programs not because the poor are lazier or more venal than other people but because everyone makes economic decisions according to what he perceives as his own best interest.

In other words, economists know that incentives (or disincentives) have to be designed into programs if they are to be efficient. On the other hand, they also know that problems of incentives, like problems of inability, are basically problems of information. And like the measures that are used to identify or target for inability, measures designed to ensure incentives can be expensive, arbitrary, or both. In a world of imperfect information, program design is an exercise in balancing the competing goals of overall efficiency, cost-cutting, and getting benefits to persons in need.

Incentive problems as a form of moral hazard

Programs in the social services may be seen as forms of insurance, and they are prone to the same problems of information that face private insurance carriers. Some of these are connected with moral hazard, which has been discussed so far in terms of an insured person's incentive to exaggerate his inability and hence claim benefits falsely or in an exaggerated amount. The insurance world also uses the term 'moral hazard' more generally to refer to the way in which insurance reduces an individual's incentive to act to decrease the risk of the insured event occurring. Most incentive problems in social programs can be viewed productively as one type or another of moral hazard.

The more general type of moral hazard can be explained in a simple mathematical model. Suppose a particular condition involves a loss to the affected individual of X dollars. Therefore, when an uninsured individual makes decisions about what measures to take in advance to avoid that condition, he takes any action whose cost is less than X multiplied by the action's reduction of the probability of the undesirable condition occurring. The existence of insurance against the undesirable condition does not change the amount of the loss itself, but it does change the individual's perception of it. If insurance transfers Y dollars to anyone with that condition, the full loss is still X, but the individual concerned perceives only his net loss, $X - Y$. Economic rationality predicts that he will take only those preventative actions whose cost is less than $(X - Y)$ multiplied by the resulting reduction in probability. In other words, insurance, which is concerned with reducing the cost of misfortune, has the perverse effect of tempting the individual to take fewer actions to prevent it (an attitude that can amount to contributory negligence[16]).

Of course, moral hazard arises only if there exist significant actions whose adjusted cost (the full cost divided by the reduction in probability of the undesirable condition) lies between X and $X - Y$. If the adjusted cost of most possible actions exceeds X, then there are few cost-effective ways for the individual to avoid the condition even when he faces the full cost. Alternatively, if the adjusted cost of most actions is less than $X - Y$, then the loss that would be occasioned by the condition is so large as to induce even an insured person to act in an efficient manner. No moral hazard exists in either case.

When moral hazard is likely to exist, program design in social insurance can provide incentives to counter it. Most obviously, $X - Y$ can be kept large, through co-insurance, user charges, and so on. If $X - Y$ is too large, however, the program may not provide benefits sufficient to meet the needs of those who do suffer the condition. Moral hazard can also be minimized by requiring those applying for the program to demonstrate that they have taken all appropriate preventative actions. Equity demands, however, that designers of social programs try to be sure that moral hazard really exists and that testing for what amounts to contributory negligence does not impose undue hardship on the claimant or others connected with him.

Examples from the unemployment insurance program can clarify these abstract concepts before we apply them to the social services. UIC benefits help protect an individual (or family) against the enormous short-term difficulties occasioned by the loss of a job. However, decreasing the harm unemployment does to an individual reduces his incentive to avoid it. Moral hazard does not exist if unemployment is caused by a fall in labour demand in the whole economy or even in a particular field or geographic area; no matter what actions the individual takes, he stands a certain chance of being among the workers who lose their jobs. In other words, he can take few actions whose adjusted cost is between X and $X - Y$. But when the individual becomes unemployed because of factors under his control (say, dissatisfaction with the job or a conflict with his employer), moral hazard may be an issue. It may also arise if the individual can influence how long it takes to obtain another job (if the cost of finding a

---

16 In law, an individual is guilty of contributory negligence under the Learned Hand formula if he omits any action that would be a cost-effective way of reducing the probability of the undesirable condition occurring. (see Posner 1977, 122).

job, which includes the value of foregone leisure time, exceeds $X - Y$, but not X).[17]

Various policies can reduce these problems, but there is always a trade-off. Reducing UIC benefits decreases the incentive to become unemployed in order to collect insurance but penalizes the legitimately unemployed. Increasing the number of weeks worked required for eligibility under the program makes it harder for casual labour-force entrants to exploit benefits but is arbitrary and a hardship for serious new workers, who may be caught in circumstances beyond their control. Disqualifying workers who leave their jobs deliberately or who do not make adequate efforts to find new ones introduces the notion of contributory negligence but such disqualification can be arbitrary and difficult to enforce. For example, how can one be sure that an individual is not trying to find a job, especially in a time of recession? Providing the unemployed with public employment rather than cash benefits would reduce moral hazard but would create its own problems (high costs, difficult logistics, and so on) and would lessen participants' incentives and free time to search for private employment.

In brief, any effective method of separating the 'worthy' unemployed from the 'unworthy' is bound to be both expensive and somewhat inequitable. One would expect the same to be true in the social services.

Accident avoidance

Moral hazard certainly exists in social service programs, although it sometimes seems more important in theory and in folklore than in real life. Many programs serve persons who have suffered some sort of accident whose probability could have been affected, at least to some extent, by the individual himself. Consider vocational rehabilitation. Some of the individuals it assists have had disabling traffic accidents. Since drivers can reduce the chances of an accident by taking certain actions (driving slowly and alertly, avoiding alcohol, and so on), it could be argued that the existence of the rehabilitation program causes drivers to be less careful. Similarly, prospective mothers can reduce the probability of certain birth defects by taking various actions (eating a proper diet, avoiding alcohol, tobacco, and other drugs, obtaining medical supervision, and so on). Therefore, it can be argued that the government's assuming some of the costs in caring for retarded and handicapped children reduces the incentive for parents to try to prevent these defects.

17 A recent and controversial article (Grubel, Maki, and Sax 1975) suggested that the 1972 changes in the unemployment insurance rules, which increased benefits and decreased waiting periods, were responsible for some voluntary unemployment. But see the response by Kaliski (1975).

One must question, however, whether moral hazard really exists in these cases. No empirical proof is possible, but the costs of permanent disability seem too large relative to the benefits in vocational rehabilitation for the program to have much influence on accident avoidance. Furthermore, it is hard to believe that almost any amount of assistance to retarded or disabled children could be sufficient to make parents more careless in preventing these defects.

These examples may sound so theoretical as to be silly, but a similar approach is actually used in some areas, particularly those involving the sexual habits of the poor. Society assumes a number of costs associated with unwanted children, including the costs of welfare and subsidized day care if the mother keeps the child and those of foster homes and adoption agencies if she does not. Since pregnancy is an avoidable risk, it is argued, society's assuming the costs of unwanted children is likely to make individuals less careful in avoiding them.

In fact, although modern folklore often bewails welfare programs' lack of disincentives for the poor to have large families, no one has ever produced evidence to support this belief. Nevertheless, the notion is implicit in some programs. And unfortunately, even if the theory is true, these program designs can end up denying benefits to children, who have certainly had nothing to say about their births. For example, Ontario currently does not increase Family Benefits payments when an additional child is born to a mother already in the program (whose eligibility requirements include there being no adult male in the household). This rule certainly discourages 'irresponsible' behaviour on the part of the mother, but it also punishes a child born as a result of that behaviour as well as all other children in the household.

This example is an excellent illustration of the most important question about moral hazard. Even when it exists, should anything be done about it? Reducing or denying benefits may increase the incentive to avoid accidents but at the cost of not awarding proper care to individuals who suffer from those that do occur. The only way to eliminate all disincentive effects would be to eliminate all programs that address any needs that can, in any way, be affected by those who benefit from the programs. This problem is a general one: almost all redistributive programs involve inappropriate incentives. Although design should be as efficient as possible, some trade-off between equality and efficiency must be accepted. The presence of undesirable incentives is not in itself sufficient to condemn a particular program.

In considering moral-hazard problems of avoidance, however, program designers would do well to examine some not uncommon causes that imply solutions. One is the possibility that prospective recipients omit economically efficient, accident-avoiding actions because of poor information, about either the means of prevention or the true probabilities of accident ('it can't happen to me'). In these cases, education might have more effect on behaviour than reducing benefits.[18]

Another possibility is that designers have not given sufficient consideration to the problem of close substitutes. Consider care for the aged. As we have seen, elderly persons who are having difficulty managing by themselves sometimes choose subsidized care in an institution because it is the only choice they can afford. Sufficient subsidies to less expensive, limited-support options – such as community-outreach and home-care programs—might reduce institutionalization for several categories of persons with serious inability.

Finally, the existence of moral hazard may indicate a shortcoming in overall programs for the redistribution of income. Consider care of the aged again. Some elderly persons would not be driven into expensive (for the taxpayer) institutions if they received cash transfers sufficient to ensure the purchase of some relatively inexpensive support services to help them live in their own homes.

Again, consider eligibility rules for welfare. A number of years ago, the United States' Aid to Families with Dependent Children program disqualified any two-parent family, even if the male wage-earner was unemployed. The result was a strong incentive for an unemployed husband to desert his family so that the wife and children might receive assistance. The response at the time was to force women, as a condition of receiving benefits, to file charges against their husbands for nonsupport. Eventually policy-makers realized that an inappropriate incentive was built into the program. No social program should encourage the desertion of one's family.[19] (AFDC has since been expanded to include two-parent families with no employed member.)

These examples also emphasize a point made in Chapter 3: in-kind programs justified by inability work best when they are accompanied by a general negative income tax. Without the safety net of an adequate income-maintenance system, no goods-specific programs can function effectively because a family may consider its survival to depend crucially on qualifying for a specific subsidy program. Yet if in-kind programs are designed to compensate for low incomes, they cannot also be designed to provide proper incentives and to insure against real

---

18 The word 'might' should be emphasized. Information on seatbelts and safety had little impact until laws requiring seatbelts were passed; information linking cigarettes and cancer has not been as effective as might be hoped.

19 The point is parallel to the one suggested by Okun: that we abhor slavery not so much for itself but because we do not believe that any individual should be in such dreadful straits that he would consider such an alternative an appealing way of feeding himself or his family (Okun 1975, 19-21). Similarly, no one should be driven to a point at which deserting one's family or having an unwanted child (to qualify for welfare) begins to look like a viable option.

inability. As the Working Party on Social Services observed: 'A major factor in determining the success of social services is the degree to which people's basic financial needs are satisfied. Social services cannot be effective if this condition is not met and further, social services cannot be an adequate substitute for an assured minimum income that covers basic necessities' (Working Party on Social Services 1974, 38-9).

Work and savings incentives

Most transfer programs, whether their benefits are paid in cash or in kind, face problems of work and/or savings incentives. The trade-offs (although not necessarily the answers) are particularly clear in straight cash transfers. On the one hand, the purpose of the program is to give money sufficient for some minimum well-being to persons who cannot earn it themselves; it is only logical, therefore, that benefits should decrease as earnings increase.[20] On the other hand, if benefits decrease too quickly as income rises, recipients who can work have very little incentive to do so.

The need to retain work incentives is an economic reality based on the need to ensure large enough benefits for those who can earn little or nothing. Take a simple model where G is the transfer to someone who earns no income and t is the rate of tax-back. If t is 0.75, the transfer decreases $0.75 for each $1.00 rise in earned income, an implicit tax rate of 75 per cent. The break-even point (the point at which the transfer is reduced to zero) is G/t. Thus, if G were $12,000 per year and t were 0.75, everyone with an earned income of less than $16,000 per year would receive benefits. Such a program, of course, would involve sums of money so large that they would be difficult to raise from those remaining to pay taxes. Yet amounts higher than $12,000 per year have been suggested as the minimum an average family needs to live in Toronto, and a tax-back rate of 0.75 is the current benefit-reduction rate in many government programs, although it is very high to preserve work incentives. If the break-even point is to stay the same, any reduction in t to increase work incentives must also reduce G.

Obviously the same problem of trade-offs exists for subsidy programs that are income-tested (or needs-tested, for that matter). As long as a user charge depends in any way on earned income, that dependence reduces the client's work incentive. Yet as we have seen, income-testing generally increases the usefulness of subsidy programs justified by need, not least because it increases the benefits available for persons with low incomes. In other words, if the tax-back rate is low enough to retain work incentives, the need to hold down costs may

20 This fall-off is called a tax-back or marginal or implicit tax, although it may, in fact, not be accomplished through the tax system at all.

substantially reduce the benefits available to individuals who earn nothing or very little.

One way to address any work-incentive problems that may occur with low tax-back rates is to separate recipients according to their ability to work. For those who are unable to work (the old, the very young, the disabled, and so on), the marginal tax rate (on unearned income, for example) may be allowed to approach 100 per cent. For those who can work, the program design can either impose a work requirement or (and this is equivalent if a job is available) combine a low level of benefits with a very low rate or even a negative one if wages are subsidized).[21]

Inevitably, any such division is arbitrary and may be unfair, especially at the boundaries. (This is not a condemnation of such a division; however, as we have seen, when lines must be drawn and information is poor, problems are bound to arise.) And work requirements are hard to enforce, a problem the unemployment insurance program has confronted. (For example, how can one be sure that an unemployed worker is trying to find a job?) Nevertheless, the approach seems a worthwhile way to optimize benefits for those in greatest need while minimizing problems of work incentives.

The problem of maintaining savings incentives is similar to that of maintaining work incentives. A number of programs employ wealth tests. For example, old people who enter nursing homes must spend any savings to pay for care. For applicants for many other programs, liquid assets must fall below a certain level before subsidies can begin.

These rules seem to provide persons who expect to require assistance with an incentive to avoid savings or even to go into debt. It might be preferable to reward savings by allowing the client to retain some liquid assets and still receive a subsidy. Perhaps the income test could impute to savings a return in excess of normal market rates; in that case, someone who remained in the program for a long time would gradually exhaust his savings, while someone who was able to leave it would do so with some assets. For example, if the test ignored income realized from wealth and instead imputed income equal to 20 or 25 per cent of wealth, the individual would have to dip into his capital (since the true yield would be below the amount imputed) but would not lose all his assets if he could leave the program soon enough. Furthermore, persons with significant capital assets would end up paying an amount equal to full cost even if their realized incomes qualified them for subsidy.

Such a program design would not be without problems, but it would maintain incentives for savings while ensuring that persons with larger assets paid a higher user charge than those with smaller or no assets.

---

21 The same two-tiered approach could, of course, also be used for cash transfers, and such a design has been proposed. (See, for example, M. Lalonde 1973, 29-34.)

Incentives for family and community responsibility
Public provision of social services may also create problems of moral hazard with regard to family and community responsibility, although it is difficult to estimate their extent or propose many solutions to them. Strictly speaking, these problems are not within the realm of the economist, but they touch it insofar as they affect decisions on who should provide care and considerations of whether government services are justified in many areas.

The tradition in North American society is that the immediate family has the primary responsibility for the needs of its members, especially those who cannot care for themselves; only when the family is unable to fulfil this responsibility does the state intervene. Yet the availability of certain public programs may provide disincentives for family responsibility, especially in light of the impossibility of designing income tests that can realistically measure the resources of an entire family. For example, whenever possible, the family has traditionally assumed the care of aged parents and of retarded or disabled members. When a single parent (or two working parents) have needed day care for young children, a close relative has often provided it, perhaps at no charge. Of course, this sort of acceptance of responsibility still occurs in many families today, often at considerable sacrifice on the part of the individuals who provide the care. Many other families are equally willing to accept responsibility but are simply not able to for logistical, psychological, or financial reasons: grown children may not live in the same town as their elderly parents; a family may not have the ability to cope with the strain of caring for an ill and/or aged person or a disabled or retarded child; a single parent may have no relatives living nearby.

On the other hand, it may be the existence of subsidized care for the elderly, the handicapped, and the children of employed single parents that induces some families to transfer their responsibilities to the state.

Unfortunately, it is not possible to measure precisely which families are not capable of caring for needy members. There is no practical way for public policy to force a single parent's relatives to offer day care. Technically, Ontario's 1978 Family Law Reform Act makes children financially responsible for their aged parents, but, in practice, the province does not investigate their incomes in determining the user charge for elderly clients. In fact, the practicality of holding the family (and especially the extended family) responsible for services and income transferred to a needy individual is not clear. Although not charging families gives them an incentive to avoid responsibility, it may be a necessary trade-off for equity and for delivering services to individuals in great need.

A somewhat similar situation exists with regard to voluntary agencies. In the past, private, community-based charities were the only providers of many kinds of social services; they still share some of the load in many areas of need. Yet it seems likely that as government moves in, many private programs may disappear

68 User charges in the social services

both because of an effort to avoid duplication of services and because charitable funds are becoming relatively less available.[22]

On the other hand, voluntary agencies have an invaluable role in the social services. They can provide services beyond those the public sector is prepared to pay for and thus respond to needs in ways not practical for government (which may fear higher costs for all recipients). Voluntary agencies can work within the context of a specific community. They can handle areas of need that are not appropriate for government (religious matters, certain types of counselling, and so on). They can involve volunteers with recipients, frequently to the benefit of both.[23]

Moreover, voluntary agencies can provide centres of power that serve as counterweights to government bureaucracy. Their activities can spur new ideas. Since they generally operate on limited budgets, their efforts at cutting costs may, by example, provide some brake on public costs. At the same time, they usually hire professionals who are committed to high-quality services and may serve as watchdogs on what is provided by government.[24]

Yet most government social services are undeniable incentives to reduce private efforts. There may be no resolution to the problem of multiplying services giving families and communities less and less reason to provide care. The breakdown of communities and extended families has left individuals in need who might formerly have been taken care of. Government has had to step in.

Although its very intervention may speed up the trend, it is not clear that any alternative exists, save to design programs that retain some incentives for families and communities to intervene. Especially one would hope that public policy would encourage voluntary agencies wherever possible as an alternative to government agencies, perhaps by offering incentives to communities without these alternatives to develop them.[25]

22 The latter phenomenon is not surprising, since some people see taxation for income redistribution as a form of compulsory charity, an attitude consistent with the donor preference literature ('I agree to redistribute some of my income as long as everyone else does the same thing').
23 An illustration can be found in the way two adjacent municipalities provide skating rinks. In 1979, the City of Toronto operated sixty-two natural-ice rinks at a cost of $400,000. North York, on the other hand, provided community groups with hoses, hockey boards, lights, and space and paid for water and electricity, all at a cost of $100,000. Community groups, with this help, managed to set up eighty-five rinks on sixty-two sites, saving local taxpayers 75 per cent of the total cost. Public inspection ensured that the local groups provided good services. (See 'Handover of City Rinks Considered', *The Globe and Mail*, 7 February 1979.)
24 For a more extended discussion of the role of charity in society, see Simon (1978).
25 So far Ontario has maintained a fair mix of public and private social services. One hopes that it continues to do so.

INTEGRATING SOCIAL SERVICES AND WELFARE BENEFITS

Another problem in the design of in-kind programs and their user charges is the likelihood of their affecting one another adversely. Individuals and families in need are often eligible for more than one social service program; if they are also too poor to meet their basic needs (as is often the case), they should also be in a cash-transfer program, as demonstrated in Chapter 3. In order to target benefits and provide work incentives, all these programs normally have tax-back rates and/or user charges that vary with income. When they interact, the results can be perverse.

The problem arises when programs are designed separately with the trade-offs for each considered independently.[26] The unfortunate result is what is often called pyramiding or stacking: the way in which welfare programs' implicit tax rates can add up, often quite drastically.

For example, imagine that a family is in a negative income tax scheme that guarantees a minimum of $5000 annually and has a tax-back rate of 60 per cent. In addition, the family receives subsidized day care for which it pays a user charge equal to 75 per cent of earned income up to a maximum of full cost of $3000. When the family's earned income is zero, its disposable income is $5000 per year. But if it earns the unremarkable sum of $6000, it pays the full charge for day care ($3000) and its negative income tax benefits fall to $1400 ($5000 minus 60 per cent of $6000); it ends up with an annual disposable income of $4400. In other words employment leaves it worse off because it faces an implicit tax rate of over 100 per cent.

In fact, Ontario does not treat day care this way, but the simple example illustrates what happens if welfare programs make no allowances for families receiving multiple benefits. A 1976 Ontario Economic Council study suggested that a family that received housing subsidies, OHIP-premium subsidies, provincial tax credit, and subsidized day care and that paid income tax would have gained little by working full time. If one family member worked a 36-hour week at $2.40 an hour (the minimum wage at that time), its income rose by only $437 because of an implicit tax rate of about 90 per cent; in some ranges of earnings, the study computed the rate as exceeding 100 per cent (Ontario Economic Council 1976, 26). In 1978, when the OEC study was updated, a family that worked 37.5 hours a week at $2.85 an hour might also have been worse off than if it had not worked at all (Ontario Economic Council 1979, 64). It is not clear what percentage of families actually participated in all these programs, but it is

---

26 Ontario's practice of assigning funds under different acts to different programs emphasizes such an inefficient approach, which is shared by many other jurisdictions in North America.

clear that programs frequently co-exist without being considered together in design. Only proper integration can prevent pyramiding.

The issue is also of concern in the United States, where recipients may deal simultaneously with several levels of government and a multiplicity of programs. Aaron (1975) and Mirer (1975) discussed various ways in which the problem might be mitigated. Basically, they concluded, *at least* one of the programs serving a given family must include consideration of the rate at which benefits in the others decrease as earned income rises. Mirer suggested various alternative ways of ensuring that tax rates do not add up: for example, varying the tax-back rate of a negative income tax to keep the overall rate below some ceiling, sequencing programs (so that countable income for any program includes net benefits from all 'previous' programs), deducting user charges from other programs, and so on (Mirer 1975).

In Ontario some programs have adopted some of these principles. For example, the programs that provide subsidized day care and subsidized housing each consider the user charge for the other as an allowable expense under the needs test, while Family Benefits are included in both as income (families that receive maximum Family Benefits pay the maximum shelter allowance as rent for subsidized housing). Since all three programs exempt the same fraction of earned income (25 per cent), the programs can function so as to keep the marginal tax rate at 75 per cent (albeit over a large range of earned income). As a family earns income, Family Benefits decline, but in many situations day-care and housing subsidies reflect no increase in net income since for each $1 of earnings, income is computed to increase by $0.75 (there being a 25 per cent exemption) but also to decrease by $0.75 to account for the decline in Family Benefits. However, since a notch exists in Family Benefits (they disappear when the family works 'full time'), the system is not completely rational. Once Family Benefits are zero, an increase in income increases the user charge for the first program (determined arbitrarily), though not for the second. Moreover, other Ontario programs (for example, subsidized OHIP premiums and the positive tax table) do not integrate as neatly.

In general, rationalization should start with all programs defining 'taxable' income in the same way.[27] One could then order the programs by their marginal tax rates on earnings.[28] The program with the highest tax rate would be first to

---

27 Such an arrangement would also be convenient. Most programs already exempt the first X dollars of earned income per month in computing the user charge or benefits. It would be easy to define X the same way in each program.
28 One would expect the provincial budget-makers to consider this order in allocating funds.

TABLE 2

Benefits under three integrated programs as income rises

Earned income	Program X benefits	Program Y benefits	Program Z benefits	Total income and benefits	Marginal tax rate (%)
$ 0	$2000	$1500	$3000	$ 6500	0
1200	2000	1500	3000	7700	80
2200	1200	1500	3000	7900	80
3200	400	1500	3000	8100	80
3700	0	1500	3000	8200	75
4700	0	750	3000	8450	75
5700	0	0	3000	8700	60
6700	0	0	2400	9100	60
8700	0	0	1200	9900	60
$10700	0	0	0	$10700	

NOTE: All three programs exempt the first $1200 of earned income. Program X has maximum benefits of $2000 and a tax-back rate of 80 per cent. Program Y has maximum benefits of $1500 and a tax-back rate of 75 per cent. Program Z has maximum benefits of $3000 and a tax-back rate of 60 per cent.

For example, suppose earned income is $4700. Subtracting the standard exemption of $1200 yields $3500 of 'taxable' income. The calculation for program X is 80 per cent of $3500, which is $2800 (>$2000), so its benefits are reduced by the maximum ($2000). The calculation for program Y is 75 per cent of $3500 minus 15/16 of $2000 ($2625 − $1875 = $750), so its benefits are reduced by $750. The calculation for program Z is 60 per cent of $3500 minus 3/4 of $200 minus 4/5 of $750 ($2100 − $1500 − $600 = 0), so its benefits are not reduced.

raise its user charge or reduce its benefits for any given family. When that program had raised its user charge (or reduced its cash benefits) to the maximum, the next one in line would begin changing its benefits. Each program would compute its reduction in benefits by multiplying its tax rate by taxable income and then exempting any benefits reduced under other programs. The exemption for other programs' reductions in benefits should not be full but the fraction t_1/t_2 where t_1 is the marginal tax rate for the program whose user charge or benefit reduction is being calculated, and t_2 is the rate for the program whose reduction is being exempted. Table 2 shows possible rates for three imaginary programs along with a sample calculation.

Although the calculation seems complicated, one expects that most tax rates could be set equal, so that full exemption would be the rule and not the exception. To ease calculation and to ensure each recipient being dealt with properly, the agency that counsels him could calculate all charges and benefits and then send them out to the other relevant agencies.[29]

CONCLUSION

In-kind programs can be essential in dealing with inability. They are necessary because of the high cost of information (that is, the difficulty in assessing inability in advance so as to handle it by cash transfers). This cost also makes any attempt to improve the effectiveness of the programs (by targeting) appear somewhat arbitrary and unjust. Many social service programs now in effect in Ontario only assist people with extreme inability while those whose inability is somewhat less serious receive little help. While this is partially the result of bad planning, in many cases it is also an inevitable result of targeting.

A basic point must be emphasized: when inability is general within an easily identifiable part of the population, it is best met through income transfers. When the inable cannot be easily identified, that fact justifies the in-kind programs. Because the inability is difficult to identify objectively, program design must incorporate various tests to target the programs to those individuals or families who need them. But here we reach a paradox. Targeting (for inability and income) improves the efficiency of goods-specific subsidy programs and limits the cost to the taxpayer. But the very lack of information means that targeting, although necessary, is inevitably clumsy and somewhat arbitrary, especially at the boundaries of eligibility, where the decision on who qualifies for subsidy (and high benefits) and who does not qualify for subsidy (and receives no benefits) is being made. In other words, the high cost of information, which recommended the subsidy program over a cash-transfer program in the first place, may make attempts to improve the effectiveness of the program appear somewhat unjust. Program design then becomes an effort to balance competing goals of efficiency, meeting all needs, and meeting the greatest need. Use of properly designed tests and careful definition of the good being subsidized (often including all close substitutes) can help achieve the balance, but perfection is probably impossible.

Much the same situation exists with regard to maintaining incentives, a problem that in-kind and cash-transfer programs share. Here, too, design can mitigate arbitrary results, but it cannot eliminate them entirely. Policy-makers should,

---

29 The proposal here is equivalent to one suggested by the Working Party on Social Services. It proposed that each client family get a single user-charge bill for whatever package of services it receives; this bill would be based on the actual total cost of these services (Working Party on Social Services 1974, 84-5).

however, give some thought to the gravity of incentive problems a particular program actually presents and to whether mitigating them will cause more harm than good to overall welfare. When it is truly desirable to maintain an incentive, the wisest course is often to fix different rates of user charges or tax-backs for different classes of recipients (say, for those who can work and those who cannot).

Finally, the integration, of programs, be they in-kind or cash transfers, is essential in rational policy design. Inefficiencies in the past have arisen in part because each program has been seen as meeting an independent need. In fact, programs must be seen as part of an overall redistribution strategy. Once that is done, computing tax rates becomes relatively straightforward.

In Chapter 5, these concepts are applied to real programs now in effect in Ontario.

5
Some social service programs in Ontario

Having considered various justifications for goods-specific subsidies, developed the theory of inability in some detail, and discussed some of the problems involved in designing in-kind transfer programs, we can now apply these general ideas to specific social service programs in Ontario. The theoretical considerations have given us a framework within which we can examine the way programs work now; more important, we can make suggestions for improvements that would increase economic efficiency and take account of what seem to be clients' real needs.

Space limitations, of course, preclude any exhaustive study of all the ramifications of any program. The focus is on the point at which the book began: setting user charges, if any. This emphasis has the advantage of being of immediate concern to policy-makers. It also forces consideration of a number of important points, such as the justification for using an in-kind transfer in a particular situation, the appropriateness of targeting devices (including eligibility criteria), problems of incentives and close substitutes, and the effects of one program upon another. It also sometimes leads to considerations of which government agency ought to set the user charge and who ought to provide the service.

Available space also limits the number of programs that can be considered in this book. The first part of the chapter discusses two subsidized services – day care for children and institutional care for the elderly – in some detail. There follow briefer reviews of a number of other services: a group of outreach programs for the aged, visiting homemakers and nurses, vocational rehabilitation, transportation for the handicapped, outreach programs for families with disabled children and several kinds of counselling.

The selection of care for the young and the old as the book's primary examples is not completely arbitrary. Both involve services that arouse strong public

Some social service programs 75

sentiment and that touch the lives of many Ontario residents. Moreover, provincial expenditures for both have skyrocketed recently — for day care, 5200 per cent in the decade between 1966-7 and 1976-7; for homes for the aged, 760 per cent in the same period.[1] These dramatic growth rates suggest that Ontarians expect government to assume increasing responsibility for what used to be the concern of the family and the community; they also suggest demographic trends that are unlikely to change in the foreseeable future. For both social and economic reasons, we would be well advised to make sure our tax money is spent as efficiently as possible.

COMMENTS ON JUSTIFICATION AND STATISTICS

The examination of these and other specific programs must be preceded by two reminders: one on the importance of the particular economic justification for a service and another on the dating of statistics.

This book's emphasis on inability tempts one to consider it the only possible justification for preferring a goods-specific subsidy to a cash transfer. The temptation is increased by the fact that almost all the social services do address various kinds of inability that vary significantly within the population. Some programs, however, can be equally or better explained by the older theories of incompetence and conventional externalities.

Determining which justification applies to a program is not only an academic exercise; it often helps determine the best approach to setting the user charge. As we saw in Chapter 4, finding the optimal subsidy rate for a need-justified program involves complicated trade-offs between reaching persons who have inability and discouraging overconsumption. The presence of externalities or paternalism may simplify the situation because either makes encouraging consumption an important goal of the program.

When externalities are present, their extent should determine the rate of subsidy. Generally, a service's user charge, as a fraction of total cost, should equal only that proportion of the benefit the consumer enjoys privately. For example, if the good provides equal benefits to the recipient and each of 499 others, he should pay only 1/500 of the cost. Hence, in programs where the externality is considerable (as in vaccination against communicable diseases), the user charge should be quite low — perhaps so low as to be best set at zero. Where

1 In 1966-7, Ontario's gross provincial expenditure on day care for children was $467,000; in 1976-7 it was $24.7 million. In 1966-7, Ontario's gross provincial expenditure on operating costs for homes for the aged was $11.4 million, in 1976-7, it was $98.0 million (Government of Ontario 1967, 1977).

most of the benefits accrue directly to the consumer, however, little subsidy is called for.

When paternalism justifies a program, the situation may be even simpler. Legally incompetent recipients often have no assets, so the question of a user charge may be pointless. In other cases, such as counselling, it may be desirable to set the charge at or near zero to encourage use of the service, which the recipient cannot value correctly. In still other cases, where the client has some competence, a small user charge may be appropriate, since the aim is to increase consumption but prevent overuse.

The second point — the dating of statistics — is a familiar problem to most researchers. Given our rapidly changing world, figures in the social services tend to be outdated by the time of publication. The data used in this chapter are no exception. They are what was available when the study was done (in general, early 1979, although some of the information on day care dates from earlier work). Most of them would be higher if the research were done today. For this sort of study, however, what matters are approximate ratios and relationships: between full costs and user charges, between incomes and user charges, between the benefits of two programs, and so on. These have changed very little in the social services in the past few years. Neither have basic program designs. Consequently, unless otherwise stated, the reader may safely assume that all dollar figures have risen (roughly, by the inflation factor) without significant changes in their relationships.

DAY CARE FOR CHILDREN

Despite the attention the press gives subsidized day care, Ontario's program is a relatively limited one that designers have attempted to target to families with the greatest need. In 1979, Ontario's working parents had to arrange for the care of about a quarter of a million preschool children; only about 10,000 ended up in subsidized places in all-day institutions.[2] Budgetary ceilings limit the number of

---

2 'Preschool' children generally refers to those between two or three and five years old, the age group served by most day-care centres. Some four-year-olds and many five-year-olds are, of course, enrolled in school, but kindergarten programs last only two and one-half or three hours, too brief a time to be useful custodial care for a working parent. It is also worth noting that children in the elementary grades generally need some day care if their parents are employed. 'Full-day' school programs start later and end earlier than most employment shifts and often do not cover the lunch period. Moreover, pupils have two-month summer vacations and numerous holidays when their parents may have to be at work.

subsidized spaces so severely that some families who qualify for the program cannot find reasonably convenient centres that have room for their children.

The subsidy program is generally limited to institutional day care, as opposed to care by a babysitter or in the informal, unlicensed centres that are run in private homes.[3] Subsidized spaces are available both in centres owned and operated by a municipality (or Indian band) or in private centres (commercial or nonprofit) that have negotiated purchase-of-service agreements with a municipality.

The full cost of the service varies with the provider and with the locale. Administrators estimate the average cost for a preschool child in a municipal centre at $18.24 per day or $3720 per year (including administration costs).[4] Costs in private centres, commercial or nonprofit, are about one-third less.[5] Infant care runs considerably higher, although few municipal centres provide it.

The province pays 80 per cent of the subsidy, up to a specified ceiling, and is reimbursed for 50 per cent of the subsidy by the federal government under the Canada Assistance Plan (CAP). The municipality pays the other 20 per cent and, by choosing the providers of care, decides on the public-private mix of subsidized spaces. To some extent, it also sets the total number of subsidized spaces available, since it may spend more or less than the maximum amount for which the province will provide 80 per cent funding.

The targeting of day-care subsidies for greatest need takes two forms: the setting of priorities for the limited number of places available in each municipality and the use of a stringent needs test.

Places go first to children whose parents have physical or psychological difficulties caring for them; this group is not numerous (most such children go into residential foster care) and is not the concern of this chapter. The other available places go to children whose parents are employed, seeking employment, or

---

3 Provincial law does not require the licensing of a day-care provider if fewer than five unrelated children are cared for in a single location. Some private-home day care (also called family day care) is subsidized, in which case it is carefully supervised (and licensing requirements for the supervisors may develop in the future). One effect of organizing this previously unorganized activity is that the cost of supervised private-home day care has risen nearly to the cost of institutional day care.
4 All statistics on municipal centres came from telephone conversations with the Metropolitan Toronto Department of Social Services on January 30, 1979. Like most day-care statistics, they are based on an average of 204 days of care per year. (The figure is calculated by assuming 50 five-day work weeks minus 15 per cent for days absent.)
5 In private centres, as of January 1979 in Toronto, a year's care for a three to five year old cost $2075 in the for-profit Miniskools, $2600 and up in better nonprofit centres (Sunnybrook School, for example, costs $220 per month).

following a course of studies. In establishing priorities for these places and for waiting lists, social workers use a rough test of apparent need that gives considerable weight to single parenthood (as discussed in Chapter 4). For any given client, getting a place in a conveniently located centre involves considerable luck as to the circumstances of other families in the area who apply simultaneously or are already on the waiting list. The rough sorting occurs only on entry into the program; once a centre accepts a child, he and his siblings keep their places subject only to the family's remaining eligible for the program under the needs test.

That test provides constant reassessment of the user charge as well as of financial eligibility. The provincially devised forms first derive net monthly income by taking total income (excluding family allowance payments) and exempting 25 per cent of earned income; unearned income (including welfare or Family Benefits payments, child-support payments to a single parent, or unemployment insurance benefits) is not exempted. From net income, the test then subtracts the various allowable expenses: food, clothing, personal items (these three are taken from a table based on family size), and actual amounts spent on utilities, housing (up to a rather low maximum in the case of rent), taxes, consumer debt, work-related expenses (mostly travel), and medical needs. The resulting figure is the amount deemed available for child care; it is divided by the number of working days in the month to obtain the per-diem charge, which may not be less than $0.75.[6]

The results of the needs test also determine if the family falls within the program's upper limits of eligibility. In 1978, the maximum permissable user charge for a municipal centre was $10.50 per day, and any parent who tested as able to pay more than $15.00 could not have a child continue in a municipal

6 As discussed in Chapter 4, this needs test results in a dollar-for-dollar decrease in the user charge (to the minimum of $0.75 per day) if the family's allowable expenses rise. It also means a $0.75 increase in the charge for each dollar earned (a 75 per cent taxback rate) and a dollar-for-dollar increase for any increase in unearned income (a 100 per cent tax-back rate).

Because of the way Ontario calculates welfare benefits, any parent who receives them ends up paying the minimum user charge for day care. A severe notch occurs, however, at the point at which a parent enters full-time employment and thus becomes ineligible for welfare. Under the needs test, the day-care fee may jump considerably at this point; given the simultaneous disappearance of welfare benefits, the family may end up worse off than it was with less-than-full-time employment.

Another problem with the needs test for day care subsidies is that it counts unemployment benefits as unearned income with its 100 per cent tax-back rate. A parent who loses a job still requires day care while actively seeking a new position. During this time, family income generally falls, but the user charge for day care does not adjust appropriately.

centre. In private centres, the maximum charge is the full per-capita cost of operating the centre as negotiated with the municipality (a condition of the purchase of service is that the full cost be charged for all nonsubsidized children).

The effects of the test are fairly severe. Most families with two working parents have incomes too high to qualify for any subsidy. Families that qualify for partial subsidy often judge the user charge to be too high and make alternate arrangements for child care. Although the municipal centres appear to offer an additional subsidy to parents who are able to pay between $10.50 and $15.00 per day, in practice their clients are at the other end of the scale. In December 1978, 74 per cent of those using municipal day care in Metro Toronto paid the minimum daily fee ($0.75), while only 2.2 per cent paid $7.00 or over. Over 75 per cent of the children came from single-parent homes.

Justifications for the in-kind transfer: two possibilities
The importance of clarity as to the economic justification for an in-kind transfer becomes evident in a consideration of subsidized day care. The service can be seen as assisting working parents and their families *or* as assisting the children enrolled in the centres. If the concern is working parents and their families, the justification, if any, is the inability created by the fact that having to provide child care during working hours effectively reduces a family's available income. If the concern is the children themselves, however, the justification is paternalism: society feels a need to transfer to children (especially poor children) in their formative years somewhat more resources than their parents either can or choose to provide.

Neither goal is particularly well served by the current Ontario program. Policy-makers must, however, decide which goal is primary because the solutions to the current program's inefficiencies differ according to which group the program is to serve.

Since the arguments involved in both instances are somewhat complicated, let us examine each justification separately, along with the economic problems and solutions it suggests. The choice of goals is not within the realm of the economist.

Day care as assistance to families
If assisting working parents is the goal of Ontario's day care program, only the theory of inability can justify subsidies beyond those now provided by the limited deduction of child-care expenses in calculating a parent's income tax. My 1977 study of day care justified those subsidies on the grounds that they help achieve optimal taxation but concluded that subsidies beyond deductibility are

80 User charges in the social services

inefficient. The argument rested on a complex mathematical model describing the choices made by an individual parent between staying home (and caring for the children) and working (and purchasing child-care services). The argument for deductibility depended on particular values for various elasticities; the model showed that the benefits of any subsidy to child care beyond deductibility could be obtained more efficiently through some kind of cash transfer (for example, by increasing welfare payments or reducing the tax rate on earnings).

This preference for cash transfers holds true even in the face of the argument that day-care subsidies allow families to escape from welfare, thereby making both the taxpayer and the recipient better off. The points used in this argument are, of course, well taken. A single parent on welfare loses $0.75 in Family Benefits for every dollar he earns; since benefits disappear entirely when the parent works full time, the implicit tax rate on earnings can exceed 75 per cent. If the parent must pay for child care on top of this, there are few incentives to work. But in any conventional economic model, reducing the extraordinarily high marginal tax rate would be more efficient than providing child care in kind.[7]

This inherent inefficiency of day-care subsidies is enhanced by some peculiar incentive problems included in Ontario's program. To keep the argument simple, let us assume that the full cost of day care is $3000 per year per child.

First, the current program design gives some false economic signals about who should enter the labour force. If an individual who can earn only the minimum wage has two preschool children for whom day care costs $6000 per year, his productivity in the marketplace is less than the loss of productivity to the household. To subsidize day care for this parent is, in effect, to subsidize his joining the labour force, which makes little economic sense.

Second, the current program subsidizes only institutional day care and thus encourages the use of this very expensive service even if a relative, neighbour, or friend would make acceptable care available at a lower true cost. For example, suppose that a reliable neighbour is willing to care for a child for $8.00 per day, but the family is eligible for a subsidized place in a centre at a user charge of $2.00 per day. Since the parent does not face the true cost of almost $15.00 per day, he is likely to choose the centre because it is apparently cheaper. (In fact, since he might prefer the services of the neighbour even if apparent costs were equal, the efficiency loss may be larger than the differences in costs.)

---

7 Although this book generally rejects the theory of donor preference, it should be noted that the superiority of selective tax reductions holds true if the policy goal is simply to induce mothers to enter the labour force (because donors endorse the work ethic).

An obvious (and often heard) objection to this point is that the care offered in centres tends to be superior to the care parents purchase from babysitters. This contention may or may not be true, but it is beside the point here. Concern for the quality of care brings us outside consideration of the goal of assisting working parents and into the (quite legitimate) area of helping children. The latter concern is the topic of the next section of this book. The point here is helping working parents, and so long as that is the only goal of policy, day-care subsidies beyond deductibility are inefficient.

An argument for subsidies on the grounds of equity is more convincing. It introduces the reality of many different families with many different needs for day care. Consider three otherwise identical single-parent families with two preschool children. The first lives close to the children's grandmother, who is available to care for them at a nominal fee of $10 per week ($500 per year). The second family has no relative nearby but can obtain babysitting from a trustworthy neighbour for $50 per week ($2500 per year). The third family has no relatives nearby, cannot find a reliable babysitter, and hence faces day-care costs of $6000 per year. In the absence of any subsidy (in cash or in kind), if the three parents work, the second family ends up with $2000 less than the first and the third with $5500 less. Given the budgets of the average single-parent families, these differences constitute highly significant differences in need. To use the language developed in this book, difficulty in obtaining inexpensive child care can constitute inability that requires higher-than-average inputs to produce a minimum level of well-being.

Moreover, these variations are difficult to identify for compensating cash transfer. How can one distinguish families who have co-operative relatives or trustworthy babysitters from those who must rely on institutional day care? If one attempted to make this distinction and set up a cash-transfer system, a family would have a large incentive to exaggerate its day-care needs when applying for the program and then, after receiving its subsidy, suddenly 'discover' a lower cost alternative. Thus, the presence of significant inability, the impossibility of obtaining information about need, the high elasticity of demand for institutional day care, and the moral-hazard problems that a cash transfer would pose all combine to make a case for a subsidy to child care. It must, however, be designed to avoid the inefficiencies that the present program incorporates.

A proposal
The most efficient way to provide a rational subsidy to day care would be to let the family make its market choice of child-care arrangements at full cost and then deduct the actual expenditure from income before calculating welfare or

tax payments. (Remember, any transfer that constitutes reimbursement or otherwise depends on actual expenditures is, by definition, an in-kind transfer.)[8]

Such a proposal can be justified on the grounds both of equity and of compensation for inability. As we have seen, necessary child-care expenses effectively lower income; the parent who earns $5 per hour but pays $2 per hour for child care should be treated in the same way as the parent who earns $3 per hour and has found free child care. Facing higher day-care costs reduces the utility of one family compared with another in exactly the same way as facing a lower wage rate. Both events are in some sense equally random, and both should be of equal concern to the welfare system and should be treated equally by the tax system.

Making day-care expenditures deductible before computing taxes or welfare benefits would also reduce the two major inefficiencies of the present system. First, parents whose child-care expenses exceed their earnings would have little incentive to work (as well they should not) because their net incomes would not rise if they did so. Second, so long as the marginal tax rate does not exceed 100 per cent, a family would have an incentive to use the lowest-cost child care available and of suitable quality, since spending one less dollar on child care would increase its taxes by less than that dollar. On the other hand, the scheme would also encourage spending more to get better care, since an extra dollar spent on child care would reduce net income and hence either reduce taxes or increase welfare benefits.

To be rational, however, implementation of this proposal must be accompanied by a significant reduction in the marginal tax rate on the earnings of both the single parent and the second wage-earner in a two-parent family. In each case, the current day-care subsidy compensates for a high tax-back on earnings; it would be far more efficient to reduce the tax-back rate.

Consider first the single parent on welfare. Currently, the tax-back rate on earnings amounts to over 75 per cent. It would make sense to reduce this to well below 50 per cent, especially for parents whose net hourly wage rate (the wage rate minus the hourly child-care charge) is low. Suppose the tax on *net* earnings (earnings minus child-care expenses) was set at 40 per cent when the net wage rate is below $3.00 and then raised with raises in net wages so as to allow the worker to keep 25 per cent of any increase. The tax rate t would then be

---

8 In so far as tax payments are concerned, this scheme could use income tax deductions similar to those used currently but with higher, more realistic maximums. Any problem of providing parents with cash in hand to purchase care could be handled by making child-care expenses an item in calculating taxes withheld by employers.

$t = 0.75 - 1.05/w$, where w is the net wage rate.[9] For example, if $w = \$5.00$, then $t = 0.54$ and the after-tax net wage rate rises to \$2.30 (from the \$1.80 he takes home when his net wage is \$3.00). Sample results of this proposal are shown in Table 3.

Tables 4 and 5 show similar schemes with different minimum tax-backs: 50 per cent and 20 per cent respectively. Notice that lowering the tax rate from 50 per cent to 20 per cent only raises the break-even point from \$10,000 to \$12,400. This occurs because calculating the tax on the wage rate allows us to include, in effect, two different tax rates: one increases relatively slowly with increases in earnings because of more hours worked; the other increases more quickly with increases in the wage rate. The second, high tax-back rate should not pose serious incentive problems since higher wage rates usually accompany more interesting work and offer the promise of further increases in wages.[10]

Finally Table 6 shows the results of a scheme similar to that used in Table 3, but with the maximum 75 per cent tax-back rate beginning at \$2.00 per hour (instead of \$3.00 per hour); to compensate, the initial rate is reduced to 22.5 per cent. This arrangement would be closer than the others to Ontario's current welfare system of applying a 75 per cent tax-back only to earnings beyond some minimum. The primary difference is that this scheme, like the others, would apply the tax-back only to earnings net of day care.

To see how this proposal would work, consider the formula used in Table 6. Suppose that the client is a single parent who works full time (2000 hours annually) for \$4.00 per hour (\$8000 per year). If the family has no day-care expenditures (say, because a relative looks after the children), it receives \$2100 in welfare benefits. Day-care expenditures reduce the net wage rate dollar for

---

9 The take-home wage would then be $(1 - t)w = 1.05 + 0.25w = 1.80 + 0.25(w - 3) = (0.6)(3) + 0.25(w - 3)$. The worker thus takes home 60 per cent of his first \$3.00 per hour and 25 per cent of any wage above this. Of course, this 'tax' applies only until the parent leaves the welfare program (assuming no full-employment notches).

10 Furthermore, parents realize that they require day-care services only while their children are young, a relatively short period. Since they do not want to be trapped in low-paying work indefinitely, few would be likely to turn down an opportunity to increase their gross wages, even if they had to accept the high tax-back until the need for day care disappeared.

The scheme does, however, present some problem of identifying the wage rate of clients who work on commission or are self-employed. They would have an incentive to inflate their hours and reduce their wage rates so as to cut the applicable tax-back rates. The solution is probably to set arbitrary limits for various types of work and to allow a maximum of 40 hours per week in computing self-employment wages.

TABLE 3

Results of a minimum tax-back of 40 per cent on wages net of day-care fees ($t = 0.75 - 1.05/w; w \geq 3$)

Net hourly wage rate	Tax-back rate	Full-time work (2000 hours) Welfare benefits	Full-time work (2000 hours) Family income after welfare and day-care fees	Half-time work (1000 hours) Welfare benefits	Half-time work (1000 hours) Family income after welfare and day-care fees
$1.00	0.4000	$5200	$7200	$5600	$6600
2.00	0.4000	4400	8400	5200	7200
3.00	0.4000	3600	9600	4800	7800
4.00	0.4875	2100	10100	4050	8050
5.00	0.5400	600	10600	3300	8300
5.40	0.5556	0	10800	3000	8400

NOTE: Welfare benefits are assumed to be $6000 if earnings equal zero.

TABLE 4

Results of a minimum tax-back of 50 per cent on wages net of day-care fees ($t = 0.75 - 0.75/w; w \geq 3$)

Net hourly wage rate	Tax-back rate	Full-time work (2000 hours) Welfare benefits	Full-time work (2000 hours) Family income after welfare and day-care fees	Half-time work (1000 hours) Welfare benefits	Half-time work (1000 hours) Family income after welfare and day-care fees
$1.00	0.5000	$5000	$7000	$5500	$6500
2.00	0.5000	4000	8000	5000	7000
3.00	0.5000	3000	9000	4500	7500
4.00	0.5625	1500	9500	3750	7750
5.00	0.6000	0	10000	3000	8000

NOTE: See note to Table 3.

TABLE 5

Results of a minimum tax-back of 20 per cent on wages net of day-care fees ($t = 0.75 - 1.65/w; w \geq 3$)

Net hourly wage rate	Tax-back rate	Full-time work (2000 hours) Welfare benefits	Full-time work (2000 hours) Family income after welfare and day-care fees	Half-time work (1000 hours) Welfare benefits	Half-time work (1000 hours) Family income after welfare and day-care fees
$1.00	0.20000	$5600	$ 7600	$5800	$6800
2.00	0.20000	5200	9200	5600	7600
3.00	0.20000	4800	10800	5400	8400
4.00	0.33750	3300	11300	4650	8650
5.00	0.42000	1800	11800	3900	8900
6.00	0.47500	300	12300	3150	9150
6.20	0.48387	0	12400	3000	9200

NOTE: See note to Table 3.

TABLE 6

Results of a minimum tax-back of 22.5 per cent on wages net of day-care fees ($t = 0.75 - 1.05/w; w \geq 2$)

Net hourly wage rate	Tax-back rate	Full-time work (2000 hours) Welfare benefits	Full-time work (2000 hours) Family income after welfare and day-care fees	Half-time work (1000 hours) Welfare benefits	Half-time work (1000 hours) Family income after welfare and day-care fees
$1.00	0.2250	$5550	$ 7550	$5775	$6775
2.00	0.2250	5100	9100	5550	7550
3.00	0.4000	3600	9600	4800	7800
4.00	0.4875	2100	10100	4050	8050
5.00	0.5400	600	10600	3300	8300
5.40	0.5556	0	10800	3000	8400

NOTE: See note to Table 3.

dollar and increase welfare benefits by 75 per cent of their cost. For example, if day care costs $2000, the net wage rate falls to $3.00 per hour and welfare benefits rise by $1500, to $3600. Thus, the subsidy rate to day care is 75 per cent; however, the family retains an incentive to cut its day-care expenses, since it receives 25 per cent of any reduction. Furthermore, the parent has no incentive to work if day care costs more than he or she can earn (since reducing the net wage below zero would not raise welfare benefits above $6000).

Notice that having welfare benefits cover only 75 per cent of all increases in day-care expenditures is the kind of compromise discussed in Chapter 4. Ideally, one would compensate fully any family that must pay a high cost for day care and provide no compensation to the family that chooses to do so despite the existence of a lower-cost alternative. But there is no practical way to distinguish the two. The moral-hazard problem of incentives cannot be eliminated entirely without destroying the purpose of the program. At least the scheme reduces the problem and avoids the current program's perverse incentive of making it cheaper for a family to use the very expensive care provided in day care-centres rather than lower-cost care provided by a relative, friend or neighbour.

Now consider the two-parent family. Once again the demand for day-care subsidies arises from the high real taxes on the working wife's earnings.[11] If the goal of providing day care is to help the working mother, the obvious rational response would be to reduce the high rate of taxation, perhaps by giving a special tax exemption or credit to working mothers whose husbands are also employed.

Both efficiency and equity also require that day-care expenses be deductible from taxable earned income. At present, they are deductible, but only up to $1000 per child per year. Raising this maximum would be sufficient if the increase brought the deduction more into line with actual day-care expenditures. (Of course, the federal government would have to cooperate in changing the treatment of child-care expenses in calculating income taxes.)

---

11 When only one parent works, the family pays taxes only on income earned beyond its personal exemptions. But when both parents work, the husband loses his wife as an exemption (or vice versa); thus, the family pays a much higher implicit tax on the wife's earnings than on the husband's. For example, suppose that the wife earns $8000 per year. Her husband loses her as a deduction, and she is essentially taxed on the whole amount of her earnings; if the tax rate (federal and provincial) averages 25 per cent, she pays $2000 in taxes. Moreover, the family loses valuable services when she enters the labour force, so its real benefit from her working is considerably less than $8000. Suppose her lost household production is worth $4000; her 'real' income is then $4000, and the tax is 50 per cent of $4000. Notice that this principle holds true even if the $8000 income is net of day-care expenditures.

In summary, by combining deductibility for child-care expenses with dramatic reductions in tax-back rates, these proposals would assist working parents who have inability that is impossible to measure. This inability is their failure to find, through no fault of their own, child care that is both reliable and low (or zero) cost. Although all moral-hazard problems cannot be eliminated, the proposals do retain incentives for parents to make efficient choices in deciding whether to enter the labour market and in making child-care arrangements.

Would these proposals cost more than the current system? Possibly yes. The current system reaches very few working parents, and any attempt to enlarge a previously restricted system is likely to be expensive. On the other hand, a reduction in the tax-back rate coupled with deductibility is likely to draw more workers off welfare and save public money. Furthermore, some parents who now use expensive institutional day care might well be induced to seek out less costly arrangements, a further savings for all concerned.

If policy-makers do not adopt these proposals, the theory of inability suggests that Ontario's present day-care subsidy should not be eliminated. The program design, however, should be changed to combat some of the current inefficiencies. First, the minimum charge should be raised sufficiently to encourage the use of alternatives that cost less than institutional care. Then, so as not to hurt very low income families, especially single parents, additional earnings should be exempted to cover the charge. Noninstitutional care should be partially subsidized (perhaps by the same fraction as care in a centre), as has been done in British Columbia. To avoid inducing into the labour force parents whose day-care costs exceed their wages, first preference for subsidized places might be given to families that have the lowest day-care costs.

Day care as assisting children

If the goal of Ontario's day-care program is assisting working parents, we have seen that inability justifies a targeted subsidy but that too high a subsidy is a poor substitute for tax-rate reductions. If the goal of the program is to assist children, however, the picture changes. A high, easily available subsidy can be a legitimate way to direct to children more resources than would normally be allocated them by their parents. The justification for this approach may be paternalism (the argument is that parents do not know the full benefits of extra expenditures on their children or that children are a separate entry in the social welfare function) or externalities (the argument is that additional expenditures on children benefit the entire community, now and/or in the future).

Judging the correctness of these arguments is not within the realm of the economist. If society accepts any of them, however, economics does have something to say about whether a particular child-care subsidy program is reaching its goal.

Clearly, a day-care program does, by its very nature, provide at least some assistance to the children in it. The logical question then is whether both the recipients and the benefits are those that best improve overall social welfare.

Let us consider the recipients first. Since the current Ontario policy targets assistance to children whose parents work at low-income jobs, it implies that these children are the ones who most require assistance. The day-care program reaches few children whose parents do not work (not even the children of single-parents who are on welfare) or children whose parents work but make arrangements for noninstitutional care. If society believes that the children who are left out can indeed be ignored, well and good. Logically, however, the subsidy should not be limited to children enrolled in day-care centres unless it can be shown that for some reason their parents care less about them than do the parents of other children. Yet it seems more likely that poor parents work because they need the money, not because they wish to escape child-care responsibilities.

The program may also not go far enough in the service it provides in kind. Studies suggest that at Ontario's current levels of expenditure, children in day-care centres may not receive much benefit beyond purely custodial care (HEW 1967). So if the policy goal of day care is to provide assistance to children, it may require a program that gives more children more help than the present one. Obviously, this could be accomplished in many ways. One is that suggested in my 1977 study: an enrichment program that would run two or three hours each day with staff-child ratios well below those of public school kindergartens. A voucher system could direct the subsidy to the target group and permit children in various situations to receive the service. Children enrolled in institutional day care could enjoy the program in the centres. Children cared for by babysitters and children whose parents do not work could receive it in neighbourhood nursery schools. All the children involved would benefit. Working parents would pay for two or three hours less care each day, a potentially significant saving for them. Unemployed parents might benefit from the break and find that it improved their parenting during the rest of the day. (Krashinsky 1977, 94-6).

This proposal makes even more sense now than it did several years ago. First, the 'real' costs to society today would be lower. Falling enrolment in the public schools means that space is becoming available that was not there in the past. Well-trained young teachers are being laid off; they might be willing to accept the relatively low wages common with the day-care field. Meanwhile, more and more children might benefit from assistance. The increase in single-parent families coupled with the dwindling of community and extended-family resources is leaving many children at risk. Enriched nursery programs may well be a social service to be encouraged by substantial subsidies.

INSTITUTIONAL CARE FOR THE AGED

When an older person can no longer care for himself in the community, he may have no choice but to enter an institution. A number of types of institutional care for the aged are available in Ontario; this section considers two major ones: residential care and extended care.[12]

Residential care is largely custodial, although it may include a small amount of medical care (less than one and one-half hours per day). The elderly who are in fairly good health receive it in old age homes, which are operated by municipalities or charitable agencies and fall under the purview of the Ministry of Community and Social Services (COMSOC). Extended care consists of custodial care plus a minimum of one and one-half hours of medical assistance. It is provided in both old age homes and nursing homes and is funded by the Ministry of Health.

In other words, the dividing line between the two programs is the arbitrary one of whether the applicant needs more or less than one and one-half hours of medical assistance per day. The full cost and user-fee structure of each program is, however, quite different.

For residential care, the full cost in 1977 averaged $17.80 per day in municipal homes and $14.66 in charitable homes. A wealth test determines a recipient's subsidy, if any. Wealth is defined as all his income, including Old Age Security and Guaranteed Income Supplement (OAS/GIS) benefits, and his assets. (To prevent the 'hiding' of assets by giving them away to relatives, the test requires a newcomer to list all transfers of assets for the three years preceding his entrance to the home.) From his wealth, a client is allowed to keep a burial allowance and $51.00 per month as a comfort allowance; all the rest must be used to meet the actual cost of care. Thus, the user charge is equal to full cost if the recipient can afford it. If he cannot, COMSOC and the municipality pay whatever subsidy is necessary; the split is 70:30 if the provider of care is a municipal home, 80:20 if it is a charitable home.[13]

---

12 Among the other common types of institutional care for the aged in Ontario is that provided in chronic-care hospitals, which is limited to persons with serious medical problems and is covered by OHIP. Although these institutions assist many elderly persons, this type of care does not enter the argument here. Neither does care in commercial (for-profit) homes, because Ontario does not subsidize places in them. Given some of the excesses reported in the United States, this is probably wise. Homes for the aged accrue so much control over residents' funds as to make profit-maximizing firms a doubtful mode of provision.
13 During 1977, 65.5 per cent of the residents of municipal homes received some subsidy, paying an average of $11.15 per day. (Overall, municipal homes collected $13.44 per

90 User charges in the social services

For extended care, the full cost is much greater; in 1977, it averaged $31.46 per day in municipal homes and $26.51 in charitable homes. All extended care is, however, subsidized. The program has recipients in old age homes pay a flat $8.70 per day, approximately the fee paid by patients in nursing homes. A larger subsidy is available to any client who needs it, but this is rarely necessary. Most of the elderly poor are eligible for OAS/GIS and Guaranteed Annual Income System – Aged (GAINS-A) benefits; their total, even after subtracting a $51.00 comfort allowance each month, is sufficient to cover a user charge of $8.70 per day.

The actual amount of the subsidy for any individual depends, of course, on the actual full cost of extended care in his particular home. The province, through the Ministry of Health, pays 70 per cent of the subsidy if the provider of care is a municipal old age home, 80 per cent if it is a charitable home.

Overall, charitable old age homes receive almost 60 per cent of their revenue in user charges under the two programs, while municipal homes receive almost 40 per cent. The higher per diems in municipal homes cause some of the difference, but most of it comes from the fact that municipal homes have over half of their residents in extended care (with its higher costs and generally lower user charge) while charitable homes have only about 30 per cent. When the province introduced subsidized extended care in 1972, the intention was not to turn municipal old age homes into nursing homes, but that seems to be what has occurred.

It is also interesting to note that neither program requires recipients' families to pay for any portion of their care, although this could be done under the 1978 Family Law Reform Act, which states: 'Every child who is not a minor has an obligation to provide support, in accordance with need, for his or her parent who has cared for and provided support for the child, to the extent that the child is capable of doing so' (Government of Ontario 1978, 9). Nevertheless, no action to collect user charges from families has been attempted, and the government forms do not even ask financial questions about the family. Some charitable homes do have a policy of pursuing the well-off families of residents for

---

resident per day.) During the same period, 41.5 per cent of the residents of charitable homes received some subsidy, paying an average of $8.12. (Overall the charitable homes collected $11.95 per resident per day.) These statistics suggest there may have been no significant financial difference between the residents of charitable and of municipal homes.

donations, but compliance is voluntary (although in certain communities, one imagines the homes can bring significant pressure to bear).[14]

Justification for the in-kind transfer
The theory of inability clearly justifies subsidizing old age care. Variations in inability are present in two forms. First, on the average, old people and young people differ in the resources they require to maintain a given standard of living. Second, old people vary among themselves in how many resources they need to achieve a given level of well-being; the person who can no longer care for himself requires far more than does the one who is capable of living in the community. The general variation between the old and the young can be measured quite easily, so it can best be handled by cash transfers; this is done through providing OAS/GIS and GAINS benefits and through special treatment under the income-tax laws. The variation in inability among old people, however, would be difficult to measure. The cost of determining exactly how much cash an elderly individual requires to compensate for his particular level of inability would be great, in large part because he would have every incentive to exaggerate his need so as to qualify for more assistance. Therefore, subsidizing the goods that the elderly with inability are likely to need is an efficient way of redistributing income to them.

As we saw in Chapter 4, a subsidy can be targeted effectively if it can be limited to a good used primarily by persons with great inability. Clearly, old age homes are used only by those with extreme inability. Most elderly people regard their independence as precious and resist entering a home as long as possible; thus institutional care is attractive primarily to those whose inability is great. However, the clumsiness of targeting makes two undesired results inevitable. First, the subsidy does not reach many elderly people who have serious inability, so they continue to live, with some difficulty, in the community. Second, some people enter a home because they require help, although they might be able to live outside an institution if assistance of a different type were available. Since institutional care is always expensive, society needs programs that can reach this latter group, who have inability but do not actually require institutionalization. Several such outreach programs are discussed later in this chapter.

---

14 The general information in this section came from discussions with Donald Malcolm, Financial Officer, Senior Citizens' Branch, Ministry of Community and Social Services. The statistics may be found in Ontario Ministry of Community and Social Services 1978b.

Subsidies to the care of the elderly may be seen as a form of social insurance and as an intergenerational transfer for which the state has assumed responsibility. Care for the old has traditionally been a responsibility of the next generation. The breakdown of the extended family and of communities may make it difficult for individual families to bear the burden of caring for their own elderly members. Social insurance, therefore, spreads the load among all the younger members of society, in a sense acknowledging the debt the whole of this generation owes the previous one.

Paternalism and externalities may also justify subsidies to old age care. The elderly have many needs that are social and psychological; especially if they are suffering from isolation, they may not be able to cope with their problems or be fully capable of judging the quality of the goods and services they receive. Society will not tolerate the results of their receiving improper or insufficient care. Hence, intervention becomes necessary.

The structure of user charges: policy concerns
Although subsidies to institutional care for the aged are clearly justified, Ontario's user-fee systems present at least two problems. One involves the method of wealth-testing individuals who enter residential care. The other is the relationship between the fees for residential care and extended care.

The treatment of assets
The problem with the wealth test for residential care is its treatment of assets. The implicit tax on both income and assets is 100 per cent (up to the point at which the recipient is paying the full cost of his care). At first glance, this seems equitable. No one in residential care is likely to be employed, so the issue of work incentives does not arise. The high rate may provide a disincentive for accumulating savings, but on the whole, this does not seem an important problem.

The 100 per cent rate may, however, end up costing the taxpayers more than it saves them in some cases. Some individuals who need residential care at some point in their lives might be able to re-enter the community at a later date. Exhausting their assets by a high user charge may make re-entering the community impossible and thus end up imposing higher-than-necessary costs on the state in the long run. Take, for example, an elderly person with assets of $15,000 who enters a home because he needs assistance after an accident or the death of his spouse. Although he cannot care for himself at the time of entrance, he might be able to leave the home later on. But suppose the home's full cost is $18 per day. Since he has substantial assets, he must pay the full amount. All his OAS benefits (minus the small comfort allowance) go towards this payment, as well as about an additional $10 a day from his assets. After two years, they have fallen to $7700 and he may not be able to afford to live on his own.

One way of remedying this problem would be to count only income from assets in determining the user charge but to accumulate any subsidy as a debt payable to the home on the individual's death. This would restrain the client from giving his assets away but keep them available for use if he re-entered the community. Alternatively, a person entering residential care might be required to transform his liquid assets into an annuity that could be collected as a user charge while he was in the home but would be available to him if he left. (Any additional subsidy could be added up as a lien on any illiquid assets.) As long as the annuity was actuarially fair, the state, on average, would lose no revenue if the individual stayed in the home.

Charges for residential and extended care

The large universal subsidy to extended care means that the user charge for the service is usually lower than the user charge for residential care. This difference violates our notions of horizontal equity; although the greater inability of the old person who requires medical care does suggest a greater subsidy, it does not require that he be charged less than someone in the same financial position who does not require costly medical care. Granted, as suggested in Chapter 4, charging less to clients who use more costly services can be justified in some circumstances as a way of reaching persons with the greatest inability. These circumstances, however, always include great difficulty in distinguishing degrees of inability. In the case of institutional care, however, it is relatively easy to distinguish which type of care individuals require. (In fact, this diagnosis is part of the process of entering extended rather than residential care.)

Another possible justification for extended care's low user charges is presumably the same as the justification for low (or zero) charges for health care under OHIP. The rationale here is that illness is an insurable and extraordinary expense that should not bankrupt the patient. However, this argument implicitly assumes that the individual will recover from his illness and rejoin the community, and hence that he will someday require more or less intact assets in order to take up his affairs again. But many people in extended care remain there until they die, as do many of those in residential care. Treating the assets of two groups differently again violates horizontal equity.

In fact, it is difficult to see what function is served by the lower user charge for extended care, except the enrichment of the recipients' heirs.

Moreover, the difference between the two user charges may have perverse incentive effects. Since the division between the two programs is an arbitrary one, they are, in some sense, close substitutes for each other, at least at the boundaries of eligibility. Therefore, if patients or their families can influence the choice between the two programs, they may tend to prefer the one that provides additional care and lowers the overall fee (especially since both kinds of care may be provided in the same institution). If those who decide on the recipient's placement are concerned about his financial position, similar tendencies exist. This is not to suggest that perfectly healthy people are receiving extended care but rather that where any flexibility exists, it makes sense not to present decision-makers with incorrect economic signals.

The differences in the two user-charge systems have undoubtedly arisen because of historical differences in Canada between programs in health and programs in social services. These differences should fade in designing programs for elderly persons in institutions. Since extended care includes significant elements of residential care, it would seem most appropriate to increase the maximum charge to its users up to that for residential care, thus providing a universal subsidy only for the medical component of extended care. If the user charges for the two types of care were equal, the subsidy to extended care would be larger than the subsidy to residential care because of the former's higher cost. Thus, equal user charges would be consistent with targeting (in fact, they would be a form of benchmarking), as well as equitable and correct as to incentives.

Neither fee structure should, of course, prevent an individual from leaving care if he is able to do so. Extended care could use a scheme like the one already suggested for residential care, establishing any subsidy as a lien against the estate of the recipient. Thus, the program might continue to charge an extended-care patient a low user charge, such as $8.70 per day, while accumulating an additional charge for residential service as a claim against him on his death.

OUTREACH PROGRAMS FOR THE AGED

Most of Ontario's resources for in-kind programs for the elderly are concentrated on institutional care. The numbers of people and amounts of money involved are large. Hepworth estimated that in 1973 about 8 per cent of Ontario residents over 65 were receiving institutional care of some sort (Hepworth 1975, 47-8). The number is undoubtedly higher today — most institutions are full and have waiting lists — and costs to the taxpayers keep going up. Nevertheless, social service administrators (and the press) are quick to point out that the institutional programs miss many poor, elderly persons, some of whom eke out their lives in circumstances of appalling misery. Moreover, demographers warn that the numerical situation will only get worse in the foreseeable future because the elderly are increasing both in absolute numbers and as a percentage of the population.

Given these circumstances, it is obviously desirable, both economically and socially, to reduce institutionalization by finding ways to deliver services within the community. Outreach programs are being tried in many jurisdictions, and the idea seems so promising that Hepworth suggested 'more supportive care services could obviate the need for long-term institutional care for all but a very small number of very sick and frail old people' (Hepworth 1975, 112).

For some time, Ontario has had a number of outreach services, including visiting homemakers and nurses (a program examined later in this chapter) and senior citizens' centres that provide, among other things, day and vacation care and meals (often meals-on-wheels). In addition, the province recently funded a large number of demonstration projects that offered alternatives to institutional care for the aged. Twenty-seven of them were funded through COMSOC's Senior Citizens' Branch and were aimed at helping fairly healthy clients stay in the community.[15] They reached some 3500 individuals at an annual cost to the province of half a million dollars or about $140 per recipient.[16] Each project provided a variety of services, such as meals-on-wheels (or wheels-to-meals), housekeeping services, transportation to appointments, shopping, and so on, visiting, help in home maintenance and personal care, day care, and recreation.

The demonstration projects employed a notched user-charge system that was income-tested. The calculation of the charge went like this: from gross income were subtracted income-tax payments and any benefits from the Canada Pension Plan, Unemployment Insurance Compensation, OAS/GIS, and GAINS. If the resulting net income was above zero and below $1000, the user charge was 10 per cent of full cost; if net income was between $1000 and $6000, the user charge was 20 per cent to 60 per cent of full cost, jumping 10 per cent with every $1000 of income; if net income was between $6000 and $13,000, the user charge was 90 per cent of full cost; and if net income exceeded $13,000, the user charge equalled full cost.[17] Since the full costs were generally not

---

15 Another, parallel group of demonstration projects under the Minister of Health were an attempt to maintain in the community elderly persons who required chronic care. These were covered entirely by OHIP.
16 The COMSOC programs were two-year projects that mostly began operating in the fall of 1977. Although they have now run their course, final statistics and evaluation were not available at the time of writing this book. The information on them that is contained here came from conversations with Dorothy Singer of the Ministry of Community and Social Services and from an interim report (Ontario Ministry of Community and Social Services 1978a).
17 This system was based on the user charges that the federal government has included in its 1975 proposal for an alternative to CAP funding for the social services.

high — the projects kept costs down by extensive use of volunteers — this scale was quite gentle except for the notches.

Justification for the in-kind transfer

Providing outreach services to the elderly in kind may be justified by the presence of inability; the programs meet hard-to-measure needs both of old people and of families who may be caring for them. Moreover, these services may be seen as correctives to some of the incentive and cost problems involved in institutional programs.

The importance of the demonstration projects' intensive use of volunteers should not be overlooked. Not only has it kept down costs *per se*; it has also provided a strong incentive for the community to exercise its responsibility to its elderly members who are in need. As noted in Chapter 4, such an incentive is highly desirable. One hopes, therefore, that future outreach programs will be structured so as to retain the incentive to involve volunteers rather than so as to encourage running them exclusively with professionals. In other words, the province should pay a set fraction of costs, rather than all of them, thus giving the providers of service a strong incentive to maintain community responsibility.

Outreach programs also seem an excellent complement to institutional programs. The latter target resources to individuals who need them the most. However, as the theory suggests, targeting is, by its nature, somewhat inefficient and arbitrary. Institutional programs give no assistance to elderly persons whose inability is significant but not so great as to require constant care; moreover, some of the elderly in institutions could live in the community with some assistance.

If the demonstration projects prove to have reduced institutionalization, continuing them might conceivably save money. In 1977 the average subsidized individual in residential care for the aged cost taxpayers about $2400 per year; if outreach projects could keep less than 6 per cent of their recipients out of old age homes, then in theory the province would save money.[18] One doubts, however, that overall expenditures would fall in practice. Most of the institutions are full, so demand probably exists for any spaces freed up by outreach programs. Furthermore, although it is difficult to estimate how much use permanent outreach programs would attract, one suspects it would be high. Many of the services offered would be attractive to persons whose inability is not large. For example, the fact that an individual can provide transportation for himself

---

18 The figure of 6 per cent represents the ratio of $140 (the average cost per recipient of the outreach programs) to $2400 (the cost to the taxpayer of institutionalization).

Some social service programs 97

does not mean that he might not prefer to have someone else do it for him. Thus, there is bound to be more use of services that are subsidized than would occur if they were sold at full cost and equivalent cash transfers given to recipients.

It must be emphasized that this overuse would be an *inevitable* result of extending the programs. The extreme targeting that results when only institutional care is subsidized works because institutional care is useful only to a limited group of people with great inability and because this care is not easily overused. When services that are useful to a larger group are subsidized, some overuse is bound to occur. This overuse does not mean, however, that outreach programs should not be adopted, only that user chargers must be carefully structured. The programs do serve those who suffer from inability and can also keep the elderly out of institutions. As we saw in Chapter 3, the greater the problem of overuse, the larger should be the user charge to discourage overconsumption.[19]

This rule of thumb must, however, be applied with discretion. For example, designers must be alert to the dangers of pyramiding if the client receives more than one service. The user-charge system employed for the demonstration schemes lowers the subsidy rate as income rises, independent of the full cost of all services received. Thus, if two clients have net incomes of $6000 and one uses services that cost $500 while another uses services that cost $1000, each pays 60 per cent of full cost. In fact, the second client has greater need and may require a larger subsidy. If the programs are made permanent, it might be preferable simply to raise the user charge to 10 per cent of net income up to full cost.

Some outreach services replace client expenditures (meals-on-wheels, for example, replaces normal food purchases); in these cases, benchmarking the minimum charge might help prevent overuse.[20] Screening by a program's administrators can also limit abuses.

On the other hand, there are some services — especially those that bring the elderly together and serve social ends — for which overuse should not be a concern. When full information is not available (because the old do not perceive their inability) or when externalities exist (usually the case in group activities), subsidies are appropriate independent of inability. Hepworth suggested that a

---

19 In terms of the model in Appendix C, even when the elasticity of demand, is significant, subsidies are still justified if the recipients have high marginal utilities of income and cannot be reached by cash transfers. However, an increase in the elasticity of demand lowers the value of the optimal subsidy rate.
20 Kosher meals-on-wheels operates in this manner; it charges a minimum of $1.50 per meal to clients who receive GAINS, and up to a maximum of $2.50 per meal to others.

'wide variety of community support services are required to ensure that old people do not become isolated and neglected' (Hepworth 1975, 158). In these cases, use should be encouraged, and it may be desirable to provide some subsidy to all users, regardless of their incomes.

These concerns are, however, somewhat premature. The demonstration projects had not yet been properly evaluated when this book was written. The optimal structure for user charges cannot be known until it is clear to what extent outreach programs can, in fact, prevent institutionalization and to what extent they are used by persons whose inability and need is relatively small.

It does appear, however, that these programs hold significant promise for reaching persons in need and that their continuance and expansion should have a high priority. In these days of budget limitations, funding new permanent programs is not popular; abandoning community outreach programs, however, would almost certainly be a false economy. If these demonstration projects have been effective, then everyone would benefit from their continuance. The recipients who might otherwise enter old age homes are better off because they prefer to remain in the community. The recipients who otherwise would not enter institutions are better off because they are able to live more successfully. The taxpayers may even be better off because costs are lower than those of institutional care.

Others ways of reducing the costs of institutional care should also be examined. Some different types of residential care have been developed to make individuals responsible for themselves as much as possible. In half-way programs, elderly participants occupy their own apartments but enjoy one communal meal each day (in a sense, centralized meals-on-wheels) and have access to various services.

Again, these programs can save money while improving the well-being of the recipients. This being a rather rare occurrence in the social services, it must be exploited to its fullest.

VISITING HOMEMAKERS AND NURSES

Visiting Homemakers and Nurses is a program designed to help families during periods of crisis and to reduce the probability of institutionalization for the elderly (roughly 70 per cent of the program's clients), the ill, and the handicapped.[21]

21 The proportion of the elderly is a rough estimate provided by Marion Langhorne, Supervisor, Homemakers and Nurses Services, Municipal Welfare Consulting Unit, Ministry of Community and Social Services. The information on the program came from Ms. Langhorne and from Ministry of Community and Social Services 1975.

Visiting homemakers provide various services for various kinds of clients. For an elderly, handicapped, or ill person, they keep the household functioning by helping with or taking over meal preparation, shopping, doing laundry and cleaning, and providing some personal care. For a client whose spouse has died, deserted the family, or is ill (at home or in the hospital), the homemaker cares for the children and manages the household so he can continue to work. Homemakers may also care for sick children whose working mother usually uses day care (centres do not allow sick children to attend). Recently, the program has begun serving some of the mentally retarded, either helping them to live on their own or providing some relief to parents with retarded children. In addition, some forty-seven Ontario municipalities employ about 250 teaching homemakers to instruct welfare recipients about care of their families.

Visiting nurses provide professional services that permit elderly, handicapped, or convalescent people to stay out of expensive hospital beds. A physician must certify that their services are necessary for the recipient to avoid hospitalization. Normally, some medical improvement must be possible for the client, but three projects now allow home care for chronic cases.

In most parts of Ontario, voluntary agencies administer both the homemaker and the nursing services. Some areas that are not covered by agencies contract with private firms to provide services. In some cases (for example, in Hastings County), municipalities run the services themselves.

The full cost of both services in 1977 was a minimum of $21.20 per day; in the major cities it was twice as much, making a province-wide average of $30.00 per day.[22]

Visiting homemakers and nurses are sometimes covered by Home Care, an OHIP project designed to economize on the use of hospitals; it carries no user charge. More often, however, the services are provided under a COMSOC program that does involve a user charge. This charge depends on both an assets and a needs test.[23]

The assets test determines eligibility for subsidy. If a family's liquid assets exceed $2500 for two adults or $1500 for one, then it must automatically pay the full cost of the service it receives.

A needs test similar to that used for the day care program determines both eligibility and the user charge. Total monthly income is computed by adding earned income net of taxes, OHIP payments, and an automatic exemption of up

---

22 In Toronto, in 1978, the Visiting Homemakers Association charged $5.65 per hour, with a minimum of four hours per visit, and the Victorian Order of Nurses and the St. Elizabeth Association charged $13.65 per visit.
23 The providing agencies do not always pass this user charge on to clients.

to 25 per cent (Toronto, Ottawa, and other major municipalities exempt the full 25 per cent) to any other income (including 40 per cent of boarder income, 60 per cent of rental income, and all pensions, unemployment insurance benefits, and separation or maintenance payments) except family allowance payments. From this total are subtracted allowable expenses, including set amounts for food, clothing, and personal expenses (taken off a provincial form) and actual expenditures on fuel, special diets, rent or mortgage payments (up to a maximum of $300), property taxes, travel to and from work (or job interviews), drugs, dentists, debt payments, and other. An extra $51 is automatically subtracted for the aged. Subtracting these expenses from income yields 'Available Monthly Income', which is then divided by 21 to determine the user charge.[24]

The municipality pays the subsidy to the provider of service. As for day-care services, the province then reimburses the municipality for 80 per cent of the expenditures, up to a ceiling, and the federal government covers 50 per cent of the total, resulting in a 50-30-20 split. In 1976-7, Ontario budgeted just under $5,000,000 for the program, and the figure was close to $6,000,000 in 1978-9.

Justification for the in-kind transfer and policy concerns

The Homemakers and Nurses program is clearly designed to reach individuals who have significant amounts of inability, which is the justification for the subsidy. Since the supplying agencies assess inability on an individual basis (in order to determine how much of the service is required), it might appear that cash transfers would be more efficient. As we have seen, however, when the supplier determines the required quantity of the need-good and when inability (and hence quantity) may vary over time, assessment for cash transfers is expensive. Visiting nurses fulfil a medical function and automatically reassess their patients as they provide the service. To a certain extent, visiting homemakers also reassess need as circumstances change; although they may not be professionals, they are experienced and the agencies supply professional supervision.[25]

24 Exactly what to divide by has been a question of recent debate. Unlike day care, which is used every working day, the services of visiting homemakers or nurses are often needed only once or twice a week. In the past, the needs test divided 'Available Monthly Income' by 30 to derive the daily user charge; for a family being visited twice a week, this meant only a third of available income was assessed as a user charge. Under the budget restraints of the late 1970s, the divisor was changed to 21, significantly raising the user charge.

25 Agency determination of need does, however, raise one problem. Since the taxpayers, rather than the agency, pay most or all of the subsidy, the latter has little economic incentive to get clients off its roles. Voluntary agencies are naturally eager to help poor clients, and one occasionally hears stories of families allowed to remain in subsidy programs for years after the extreme inability has disappeared. This can only happen when user charges are zero or very low.

In the case of homemaking services, inability is partly determined by how much assistance a client has available from family and friends. This availability cannot be established objectively, a fact that helps to justify the subsidy. The same fact also underlines the general desirability of a user charge for the program; appropriate user charges encourage family and community assistance, while equivalent cash transfers would provide a disincentive. The wide variations in inability also suggest the inefficiency of the current practice of giving full subsidies to persons whose incomes are very low. In general, it would probably be more efficient to give these recipients a combination of a higher cash transfer (since their need can be partially measured) and a higher user charge.[26]

Another fact is of greater concern. The program serves a number of distinct groups, some of which should be treated quite differently from others in determining the optimal user charge. The key differences among these groups are the relative difficulty of assessing the degree of inability, the likely degree of overuse, and the elasticity of substitution for the subsidized service.

Elasticity of substitution is crucial but complicated in considering the Homemakers and Nurses program. We have already seen, both in theory and in the examination of the day-care program, that subsidizing one commodity without subsidizing close substitutes results in inefficiencies. For homemakers' and nurses' services, each group of clients has different alternatives. Many of these substitutes are also subsidized, but under different programs — sometimes even a different provincial ministry — and the user-charge systems take no account of each other.

Consider first visiting nurse service for clients under the age of 65. It frequently enables patients to stay out of hospitals, so in a sense it is a substitute for a service fully subsidized by OHIP. The full cost of a nurse's visit is decidedly less than the full cost of a hospital bed, but imposing a user charge for this service only provides patients with a faulty economic signal to stay in an institution. Similarly, visiting nurses frequently provide the elderly with an alternative to entering a nursing home, where subsidies of $600 per month and higher are common. Therefore, it hardly seems appropriate to provide a high subsidy for visiting nurse care only if the elderly recipient has a very low income. Moreover,

---

26 Two unfortunate results of the assets test must also be noted. Testing for liquid assets only penalizes renters over homeowners, who can easily tie their assets up in a mortgage. Second, as noted in the discussion of institutional care, a strict assets test can destroy a client's ability to recover from a crisis since he must reduce himself to poverty before he can receive help. Surely a preferable design would impute an income to assets (perhaps at an interest rate in excess of the market) and simply include that figure in total income.

in both situations, the nurses provide constant professional reassessment of need, so overuse is unlikely, and no user charge is needed to prevent it.

Now consider visiting homemakers. When they assist the elderly, the service is an outreach program like those already discussed. To the extent that it enables the elderly to live outside expensive institutions, significant subsidies are in order. On the other hand, the service may appeal to individuals whose inability is not great. Some user charge may be necessary to discourage overuse (although overuse cannot be regarded as a serious problem once one compares the service to high-cost institutions).

Now consider the other kinds of clients visiting homemakers serve. For the disabled person whose expenses are extraordinary and who needs a homemaker in order to live outside of an institution, a minimal user charge seems appropriate. In this case, the inability is extreme and the alternative is heavily subsidized care in an institution.

On the other hand, for the working father whose wife has died or deserted, the homemaker is a replacement for day care and the user charge should be set equivalently or even higher so as to induce him to search for alternative arrangements. For the working father whose wife is ill, the homemaker is, in a sense, a medical expense and ought to be insurable, although to prevent overuse, co-insurance (a user charge) should be imposed.

The point is that different systems of charges seem to be appropriate for different groups of clients. Some recipients need to be discouraged from overuse; others need incentives so as not to choose more expensive substitutes.

Unfortunately, the situation may not be easy to remedy because it is symptomatic of a deep problem in Ontario's social programs. They are designed, administered, and funded by function. Medical care falls under the Ministry of Health, residential care for the aged under COMSOC's Senior Citizens' Branch, Homemakers and Nurses under COMSOC's Municipal Welfare Consulting unit, and so on. Yet all three programs (and many others) may serve a single elderly person. The Working Party on Social Services suggested that this 'fragmented view of the individual' may lead to a person in need being served by a variety of programs, none of which addresses his real problems: 'The proliferation of specialized agencies often results in two or more similar agencies becoming involved with the same individual or family. The term multiproblem family has been used to describe this phenomenon, but it is really a problem caused by too many narrowly-defined social service programs and agencies, all dealing with the different parts of the same person or family' (Working Party on Social Services 1974, 40).

Obviously, if the different programs serving a particular group employ different systems of user charges, they may result in an inefficient mix of services as well as in pyramiding of implicit tax rates. Moreover, the optimal charge for one group that uses a particular program may differ from the best charge for other users who have very different types of inability. The design of charges for one group can be done most efficiently by the department that administers other programs for the same group.

VOCATIONAL REHABILITATION

If an adult suffers a disabling injury, he is frequently incapable of returning to his old job or profession, but unless he is very wealthy, he may not have the resources to retrain himself. Ontario's Vocational Rehabilitation program provides retraining for any such individuals who can be rehabilitated and who are not covered by workmen's compensation or war veterans' programs.

When a person enters the program, experts first assess his disability and potential for rehabilitation.[27] He receives vocational counselling to help him determine an occupational goal, and he then participates in working out a program to achieve that goal. There is almost no limit to the training and supports that the program can provide: tuitions, books, any essential devices (artificial limbs, wheel chairs, tape recorders, special texts), an attendant or aide, transportation, and so on. All these benefits are counted as essential to retraining and are fully subsidized.

The program may also provide the recipient with a maintenance allowance. Eligibility for it is needs-tested; the client cannot receive maintenance assistance while he has liquid assets (including any insurance settlement) in excess of $1000.

Both parts of the Rehabilitation program continue as long as the recipient needs schooling or training, even if this period stretches to many years.

In 1976-7, the program provided individualized retraining for about 13,600 disabled persons. Its costs ran some $2,900,000 for maintenance allowances and $6,200,000 for tuitions, supplies, and other necessary services. The previous year it had 'graduated' about 900 persons into competitive jobs at an average annual salary of $10,000.[28]

Justification for the in-kind transfer and policy concerns

Injury or accident creates a large amount of inability, but assessing that inability before counselling and training is almost impossible. Only during the rehabilitation process does it become clear just what amount of training can benefit the client. Thus it would be impossible to calculate cash transfers to compensate for

---

27 Persons who cannot be trained sufficiently to enter the labour market directly may go into sheltered workshops. Those who cannot be rehabilitated receive welfare benefits.
28 Most statistics in this section were supplied by Peter Crichton, Rehabilitation, Ministry of Community and Social Services.

inability and then charge those in rehabilitation for the service. Also, the elasticity of demand is virtually zero. No one would deliberately disable himself in order to qualify for rehabilitation. Moreover, a disabled person usually desires as much rehabilitation as is practical; a lack of this desire can be viewed as incompetence, which also calls for a highly subsidized in-kind transfer. Thus, a rehabilitation program is a prime candidate for an in-kind program, and zero user charges are appropriate.

The questions for policy lie not in Ontario's rehabilitation program but in its overall treatment of the disabled. Again, the issue is the government's division of responsibility by function rather than by recipient. A disabled person qualifies for Guaranteed Annual Income System – Disabled (GAINS-D) only if he is permanently disabled, so technically someone who can benefit from vocational rehabilitation may not qualify for GAINS-D. On the other hand, a disabled person may qualify for Family Benefits, but only if he does not work full time. As long as he is in the Rehabilitation program, he receives whatever help he needs, but when he finally graduates, he loses his benefits. Theoretically, he can now live on the income from his job, but a starting salary, even for full-time work in a professional field, is often not enough to support a seriously handicapped person, who may require very expensive aids (such as a full-time attendant) in order to get dressed, keep house, shop, and so on. To obtain the services he needs, he may be forced to enter a nursing home. Here he may encounter circumstances that make it difficult or impossible to work.[29]

Such institutionalization is, of course, undesirable for a number of complementary reasons. As Hepworth stated: 'Institutions generally are in disfavour, partly because their custodial or holding functions have begun to seem irrelevant to the needs of their residents, and partly because they are expensive to operate. A whole new set of circumstances is combining to accentuate the need of the handicapped both to live in the community and to be adequately supported and cared for when they do so' (Hepworth 1977, 13). Maintaining the rehabilitated but handicapped person in the community benefits both the client and the taxpayer, but it requires services beyond rehabilitation.

This concern was expressed by the Working Party on Social Services in commenting on the Vocational Rehabilitation of Disabled Persons Act: 'Shareable services emphasize restoration, training and placement but do not include adequate follow-up and employment support services. Services to *maintain* employment are not provided for in the Act and Agreement, thereby weakening the

---

29 For example, one disabled man in a chronic-care hospital found that he could not work because the schedule in his institution did not enable him to be dressed and ready to leave in time in the morning (Tesher 1979, C1).

preventive and supportive role the program could potentially play' (Working Party on Social Services 1974, 60).

It is not that the disabled person, rehabilitated or not, has no help available to him. He is eligible for the Homemakers and Nurses program, which can assist him considerably. (Depending on his area and its funding, it may even pay for live-in help.) Transportation subsidies (discussed below) are a useful innovation. Perhaps even more useful may be a demonstration project titled Housing and Support Services for Handicapped Adults but more often called Care Package. A combined effort of the Ministry of Housing and COMSOC, it provides special subsidized apartments *and* support services to persons who would otherwise have to live in institutions. Although the project is currently very limited (to 75 housing units) and most of its clients have been recruited from nursing homes or chronic-care hospitals, there is no reason why it could not be expanded and used to assist employed disabled persons.[30]

The point is that although services useful to the disabled are available, they are not co-ordinated with each other. Moreover, most programs for rather general use are designed for persons who are normal but poor. For example, the user-charge formula for Ontario Housing Corporation (OHC) units takes no account of the range of commodities a handicapped person may need in the course of each day. And since its income test is geared to the poor, it does not accommodate middle-class spending on clothing, food, and entertainment, although some such expenditures are often necessary to advance in a profession. Even the principle of the user-charge design is often inappropriate for the disabled. For example, one hopes that a normal client will eventually earn enough to pay the full cost of OHC units and then to leave; for many of the disabled, leaving the program may never be possible. Thus, it is not appropriate for the handicapped to be subject to the same income test as the normal person, especially if the program's user charge is one that essentially takes all income beyond some minimum.

The solution to this problem would not require a radical restructuring of responsibilities, with all the high political and other costs of such a change. Suggesting that all services for the disabled must be co-ordinated is not equivalent to suggesting that one department should be responsible for all these services. Having five groups hiring visiting nurses would be no more desirable than having one department dealing with five different groups in need. Just as the problem of pyramiding can be solved by setting some interprogram rules, co-

---

30 The information on the Care Package came from Dave Pitt, Coordinator, Group Homes and Halfway Houses.

106 User charges in the social services

ordination just requires interprogram adjustment of user charges and interdepartmental co-operation in program design. For example, COMSOC's Rehabilitation branch could be made responsible for the physically disabled who have re-entered the labour force. If a client needs a visiting nurse and/or homemaker, the service would be provided by the Homemakers and Nurses Service department, but the Rehabilitation branch would designate the user charge.

The disabled are usually eager to re-enter the work force (work being most adults' link to the rest of the world), and their earnings are a net gain to society. In 1977, the Care Package cost about $32.50 per day, an amount comparable to the cost of nursing-home care. If its recipients were working at productive jobs, its costs would decline while the disabled were made better off. The economic and nontangible gains would be great.

TRANSPORTATION FOR THE PHYSICALLY DISABLED

In order to get to and from work or school, run errands, go to the doctor, and so on, a seriously disabled person who lives in the community may require transportation in a specially designed vehicle that can accommodate wheelchairs (and often attendants). Such service is available privately at full cost, but a recent pilot project called Wheeltrans has begun to offer subsidized trips in Toronto, Ottawa, Chatham, Sault-Ste-Marie, and Peterborough. Funded half by the municipalities involved and half by the Ministry of Transportation, the service is seen as a substitute for the public transport that recipients cannot use.[31]

The Toronto program is the largest but typical of those in other cities. The Toronto Transit Commission (TTC) contracts for services from Wheelchair Mobile, a for-profit firm that also supplies other programs of transport for the disabled.[32] It uses vans to provide curb-to-curb transportation (including assistance in and out of the vehicle) on two different services. One is a subscription service that carries the handicapped to and from work and school in groups; the provider arranges these regular runs as efficiently as possible. The other, nonsubscription service answers calls for the handicaps' other transportation needs; since the trips are variable in timing and duration and since demand may outrun the vehicles available on any particular day, it uses a priority system. Trips for medical purposes (60 to 70 per cent of the nonsubscription trips) and for getting

31 Other transportation services for the handicapped in Ontario include those subsidized by school boards for disabled students, by the Vocational Rehabilitation program for its clients, and by service organizations such as the Rotary Club. Many of these programs have contracts with the same provider of service.
32 The information about Wheeltrans came from David Reiner of Wheelchair Mobile.

to work receive first priority; trips for shopping, banking, or social visiting are given lower importance. The priority system, high demand, and Wheelchair Mobile's attempts to fill the vans to capacity on efficient routes mean that any nonsubscription call may or may not be answered at the time requested or at all; Wheeltrans officials suggest that this uncertainty may discourage some eligible riders from using the program.[33]

All handicapped residents of Metropolitan Toronto are eligible for the service, and about 5000 persons are registered for it. An applicant proves eligibility by providing a doctor's letter that describes his handicap and testifies that he cannot maneuver on a regular TTC vehicle. There is no income test.

The full cost of the service is about $14.00 per hour; Wheelchair Mobile estimates it can make nearly two trips per hour, which works out to a full cost per trip of between $7.00 and $8.00. Users pay a flat, benchmarked rate of two TTC tokens or their cash equivalent (about $1) per trip. Wheelchair Mobile receives a subsidy of $11.78 per hour, so the subsidy rate is around 80 per cent or higher.

The approximate subsidy rate can also be derived from the statistics on use and budget. In 1977-8, the service handled an average of 400 people on each of the approximately 250 week days, transporting 100,000 people during the year at a cost to the taxpayers of about $750,000. This $7.50 subsidy per trip compares with a user charge of approximately $1.00.

Justification for the in-kind program and policy concerns
In the Lancasterian consumption function explained in Chapter 3, the disabled have to purchase more inputs than other consumers to produce any characteristics that require transportation. Thus 'good health', 'meals', 'earning a living', and 'social visits' all require unusually high expenses for trips to the doctor, shopping, commuting, and getting to friends' homes respectively. This clearly constitutes inability. Furthermore, the inability varies widely (how many trips to the doctor are needed? will stores in the neighbourhood deliver? how far is it to work or friends' homes?) and depends partially on the availability of potential assistance from neighbours, friends, or relatives. Thus, it would be expensive to identify for cash transfers, which, in any event, would give the recipients incentives to exaggerate their inability.

Clearly then, inability justifies the in-kind transfer. Moreover, as discussed in Chapter 4, the service is truly useful only to the inable and so is easily targeted to them, a fact that makes the program's very rough screening appropriate.

---

[33] This situation was improved recently by expanding Wheeltrans' budget, allowing it to add vans and make nonsubscription service available evenings and weekends.

What is less clear is whether the subsidy rate should be as high as it is. The current benchmarked user charge is an attempt to compensate more or less exactly for inability (that is, to charge an inable person an amount roughly equal to what able persons pay for the same end product), but it may encourage overuse among the inable. With transportation available at a low cost, clients may tend to take more trips than they would if given equivalent cash transfers and faced with the full cost of the service. Furthermore, if they faced the full cost, they might be more likely to arrange alternate methods of transportation (with relatives and friends) if possible. In other words, the current design of the user charge involves a trade-off: it accepts the inefficiency of possible overuse in order to increase the degree to which the program can compensate for the inability.

In defence of the high subsidy rate, it should be noted that the service's potential for overuse can be exaggerated. For many of the disabled, any trip is likely to involve a significant amount of planning and exertion, so the elasticity of demand may not be very high. Furthermore, the program does use a rough technique for limiting overuse. As discussed in Chapters 2 and 4, limiting the quantity of the subsidized good that an individual may receive can limit or eliminate overuse. This is the effect of the program's priority system; low-priority trips are not as subsidized, since the service is not always available. If policy-makers think further limitation desirable, the program could also easily employ differential charges: a low one for certain trips (to and from work or school, to and from the doctor) and a higher one for shopping, visiting, and so on. To avoid discouraging all low-priority trips, the design could allow each recipient a certain number of trips each month at the lower rate.

The high rates of subsidy can also be justified as part of an outreach effort to keep disabled persons out of institutions. If, for example, a disabled person who is living and perhaps even working in the community cannot afford special transportation to and from his home, the alternative may be full-time care in an institution, at much higher cost to the public.

Finally, the lack of an income test is appropriate for this program because it is unlikely to be used by the wealthy, who prefer more private and reliable service.

OUTREACH PROGRAMS FOR FAMILIES WITH DISABLED CHILDREN

Children who are physically disabled or mentally retarded may be cared for in institutions, but maintaining them in their own homes is frequently desirable for both social and financial reasons. Doing so is, of course, very difficult for parents, and a number of programs have been developed to assist families who choose this course.

Among these are a number of outreach programs funded by the Community Resources Branch of COMSOC. The Infant Stimulation program teaches parents how to stimulate and help children under the age of two. The Behaviour Training program, which deals with children over the age of two, attempts both to help children directly to modify their inappropriate behaviour and to help parents learn to cope with and teach their children. A Family Support Worker program provides a family with someone who can help coordinate the many services available for a developmentally handicapped child. Parent Relief programs allow the parents to get away temporarily by providing help for a few hours, for weekends, or for vacation periods; the child may be cared for in a centre, by a babysitter or homemaker trained to care for retarded or disabled children, or by a host family that has volunteered to associate itself with specific children over a period of time.

In general, all these programs employ only nominal user charges.[34]

Justification for the in-kind transfers
Outreach programs for families with handicapped children can be justified by the model of inability. A disabled or retarded child imposes such tremendous costs on the family, both financially and socially, that there can be no question about the presence of inability. Obviously, too, the inability varies significantly. Most families do not have to cope with these problems; those that do vary among themselves both in the problems they must face and their psychological and financial ability to handle them. Although it might be technically preferable to give the family a compensating cash transfer, it is difficult to assess the magnitude of its inability, which may vary over time (for example, parents may need relief at some times but not at others). In-kind transfers provide assistance when inability is high.

The decision to pay benefits in kind is also based on moral-hazard considerations. These families are usually under much financial pressure, and the incentive to exaggerate need might be strong if cash compensation were available. Moreover, the measurement of need (the child's, the family's, or both) is part of the process of many of these programs. And as we have seen elsewhere in this book, when professional assessment of need is part of the service, in-kind benefits are generally superior to cash transfers.

---

34 The information on the programs came from Maxine Walsh, Resource Officer, Special Projects, Community Resources Branch, Ministry of Community and Social Services.

Significant user charges for these programs would be inappropriate. Overuse is limited by supplier and by the parent's desire to care for the child. Moreover, the alternative to these services is often institutionalization, at a far greater cost to taxpayers.

COUNSELLING SERVICES

A number of counselling services are funded through COMSOC. In a sense, the initial part of the Vocational Rehabilitation program is counselling; so is the work of the homemakers who teach welfare recipients how better to manage their homes. Two others are welfare counselling and debt counselling.

Welfare counselling assists clients with various kinds of problems and refers them to others for help. It is available without charge to persons who qualify for Family Benefits or General Welfare Assistance. In Toronto, the program is administered by nine different agencies, including the three local Family Service agencies. They bill the government in a number of different ways, but in general collect somewhat over $20 per interview; the total annual cost in Toronto is just over $200,000.[35]

Debt counselling is a COMSOC demonstration project. The actual counselling is done by twenty-nine independent agencies across Ontario (about twenty are Family Service agencies, the rest independent credit-counselling agencies), who provide 40 per cent of the funding. The remaining 60 per cent comes from the project, which had a 1978-9 budget of $708,000. No fee may be charged to clients, who are accepted without any income test. The only eligibility requirement is that the applicant's income, after meeting his needs, must be insufficient to satisfy his contractual obligations to creditors; in fact, most clients are being sued for their debts.[36]

The average client has a gross annual income of about $10,500 and outstanding debts of $8000. When he first goes to the agency, it studies his financial position. It may find that budgetary advice is all he requires. In other cases, the client goes through a process known as 'Orderly Payment of Debt'; he is allocated a portion of his income sufficient to cover his needs, and the agency divides the rest of it among his creditors, according to a plan it has worked out with them.

---

35 The information on the program came from Walter Warrener, Supervisor, Toronto Social Services Department.
36 The information on debt counselling came from Ron Mason, Program Consultant, Credit Counselling.

Some social service programs 111

In 1977-8, the program handled about 13,000 cases and closed 58 per cent of them, three out of five with full or partial success. Rarely were creditors uncooperative. The total cost of the program in 1977-8, including the agencies' share, was about $1,000,000 or $78 per case. As a percentage of cases closed successfully or partially successfully, the cost was $222.

Justification for the in-kind transfer
All various counselling programs mentioned are designed to help clients improve their well-being and can be justified by the presence of inability. As noted in Chapter 2, some people are more efficient consumers than others, and those who are the worst consumers have the largest inability; counselling helps them get more utility for their dollars.

Paternalism is another justification. Someone must judge which families are not as efficient as others. The criteria are generally ones that many of the recipients themselves accept — at least after counselling. Before the fact, however, many clients are not aware of their need for the service.

Even if clients are aware of their need for counselling, cash transfers would not be an efficient means of meeting it (for debtors they would probably be counterproductive). There is no clear way to measure a family's inability until the counselling actually takes place. Furthermore, giving unconditional cash transfers to those who require counselling would create grave moral-hazard problems. And since counselling is of little use to those who do not have this particular inability, and since overuse is limited by the relatively low value of surplus units of counselling and by the fact that the counsellor decides how much of the service is consumed, in-kind transfers are generally superior to cash transfers as a way of addressing counselling needs.

Whether inability or paternalism justifies subsidized counselling programs, user charges for them are generally inappropriate. The individual is often not aware of his need, at least until the situation becomes serious, so the problem is not deterring overuse of counselling but encouraging early use. The programs are relatively inexpensive relative to the costs of the problems that give rise to the need, and any savings in costs that a user charge might effect would be offset if it discouraged prospective clients who require it. This judgement must, of course, be made on a service-by-service basis, but it is likely to be true more often than not.

On the other hand, possibilities for alternate financing exist, at least for some types of counselling. In the case of the debt counselling program, the cooperation of creditors suggests that they might be prepared to pay a fee for successful conclusions to difficult cases. In 1977-8, the service closed 2600 cases successfully; if the debt involved in each was $6000 (below the average), then charging the

112 User charges in the social services

creditors 6 per cent of debts collected would have paid for the service. Of course, many successful cases may involve only advising the clients about budgeting, and in these cases, no fee could be collected from creditors. One administrator, however, has estimated that a 15 per cent charge might fund most agencies;[37] a smaller charge, which would share the costs between agency and creditors, might be appropriate.

Ideally, counselling would occur informally within communities and families. Realistically, the state must assume some of these functions, but some sharing of responsibility with voluntary agencies, which can mobilize local volunteers and funds, remains desirable. In this area, as in many others, the provincial government's most important function may be to reinforce and encourage local involvement and community action. Abandoning counselling services, however, would be likely to generate more costs, private and public, than it would save.

---

37 This estimate comes from Ron Mason, see note 36.

6
Conclusions

Fighting poverty consists of first measuring the gap between the resources an individual (or a family) has and the resources he requires to reach the standard of living society sets as a minimum, and then devising policies to eliminate that gap, paying due attention to the need to retain work and other incentives. When that gap can be easily measured, the economist's solution to poverty is straightforward: cash transfers dominate goods-specific subsidies because a competent consumer is best able to judge what goods and services he himself requires, and because goods-specific subsidies generally lead to overuse of the subsidized commodity and hence to losses in efficiency. When the gap cannot be easily measured, however, determining the appropriate cash transfer becomes very expensive, and an in-kind transfer may be more efficient.

Sometimes the cause of the gap is simply low or zero income. Sometimes, however, the cause is inability, a phenomenon that is at the heart of the theory developed in this book. Because of circumstances beyond their control, some competent consumers cannot take the same amount of inputs as can average consumers and transform them into the same level of well-being. When this deficiency increases the resources an individual (or family) requires to achieve minimum needs, as opposed to wants, it has been labelled as inability.

Clearly, a significant amount of inability can cause poverty even for an individual with a fairly high income. Clearly, too, inability must be compensated for − in cash or in kind − if the individual concerned is to escape poverty. Once again, the appropriate method of compensation depends on the ease of measurement. Certain inabilities cannot be easily measured in advance of consumption. Attempting to compensate for them by adjusting cash transfers runs up against the high costs of measurement and often against incentives for the potential recipient to exaggerate his inability so as to increase the money he receives because of inability. In these cases, in-kind transfers may save the taxpayers money.

The argument may be seen in terms of information costs, which are a friction or transactions cost in the system. If information were free, then each individual's inability could be determined without cost and included in the determination of his tax or benefits under a cash-transfer system. But information is not free. In some situations, it is inexpensive enough for cash transfers to retain their basic superiority. In other cases, the cost of information is so high as to make a determination of inability very expensive; then subsidizing the good required to compensate for inability may be the most efficient way of countering it. This is particularly true if persons with inability tend to consume a higher than average amount of the need-good. The subsidy economizes on information by allowing those with inability to self-select (by consuming the good in question).

Several conditions must hold for inability to justify in-kind over cash transfers. First, within any group of consumers with similar incomes, those with greater inability (and hence lower utility) must generally consume more of the good or service in question. Second, the amount of inability any individual suffers must not be measurable for compensation by unconditional cash transfers without considerable expense and without providing considerable incentive for the potential recipient to attempt to mislead the measurer. Third, the elasticity of demand must be small enough so that considerable overuse (and hence inefficiency) does not take place. In the extreme, the case for subsidy is strongest when the good or service to be subsidized is not at all useful to persons who have no inability and is most useful to those whose inability is greatest.

It should be emphasized that most basic needs can be easily measured in terms of dollars. Everyone needs housing, food, and clothing, but minimum requirements vary primarily with family size and composition, information that is easy to determine. Furthermore, demand for these goods is highly elastic. For these basic needs then, cash transfers are most efficient and in-kind programs waste resources. On the other hand, there remain a variety of needs, including many in the health and social services, for which inability is important but cannot be measured easily, and for which either demand is inelastic or quantity is supplier-determined. For these needs, cash transfers are ineffective or very expensive and in-kind transfers are preferable.

In brief, cash transfers must remain the backbone of any antipoverty program, but the optimal policy must also include a wide variety of in-kind transfers. To rely solely on in-kind subsidies would involve the government in costly and inefficient programs, but to rely solely on cash transfers would neglect significant variations in inability within the target population.

Conclusions 115

Other motives, including paternalism and incompetence, also play a role in explaining a number of subsidy programs. They cannot, however, justify many in-kind transfers for which policy-makers see a need. Adopting the concept of inability developed in this book permits reasonable explanations for a number of in-kind programs and also allows the analyst to draw the line between areas where in-kind programs are appropriate (medical care, services for the old and the disabled, perhaps child care) and areas where in-kind programs are clearly inefficient (food, housing, clothing).

Furthermore, if one accepts inability as an explanation for many in-kind programs, it clarifies some of their common features. In many cases, it is efficient to try to limit the recipients of the subsidy to persons who have the most inability (and hence most need the good in question) and to those who are most likely to be poor. The first can be accomplished by subsidizing only those goods or services used by persons with great inability, while the second can be done by income-testing. But this targeting must use arbitrary and often clumsy rules to hold down information costs. Thus, what is sometimes seen as unfairness in the system is often simply the inevitable result of attempting to target the subsidy to the group that needs it most.

On the other hand, designers can often improve targeting rules as information flows change and as they see the results through experience. For example, a concern about the pyramiding of implicit tax rates emerges from experiences with recipients eligible for a number of programs. The same experience suggests that user charges should be structured more by recipient group than by social service, and that recipients from different groups who use the same service may properly face differently structured charges.

The examination of specific programs in Chapter 5 suggested several other general points. First, simply subsidizing expensive services for persons with great inability may be inefficient if some of the target group have cheaper substitutes available in the community. Therefore, program designers must carefully define exactly what services are to be subsidized and how different subsidies are related.

Second (and this flows from the previous argument), policy-makers should consider expanding outreach programs. Restricting subsidies to programs provided in institutions is a way to target funds to persons with great inability, but institutional care is often both very expensive and socially undesirable. Institutions will probably always be necessary for some clients, but a wide variety of needs can be met in the community. Designers, however, must pay careful attention to outreach programs. To discourage overuse almost all clients should pay some user charges for them, but because many individuals naturally receive multiple services, much attention must be given to preventing pyramiding and to other ways in which programs can be usefully integrated with each other.

Third, the arguments above suggest that a comprehensive antipoverty program, including some form of negative income tax, is a prerequisite for properly designing user charges. For various reasons, not the least of which is avoiding overuse, all consumers, no matter how poor, should pay some user charge for certain services. This is not practical unless a cash-transfer system provides the poor with enough income to pay those charges.

Finally, it must be emphasized that user charges are not the only way to restrict overuse. In many services, the providers of service place some natural limits on demand. Also, while user charges are generally appropriate for subsidized services justified by the theory of inability, charges may be inappropriate when the justification is paternalism or externalities.

To summarize, the theory of inability rests primarily on the high cost of acquiring information about the specific problems faced by individual clients or families. Once one introduces information costs, it becomes difficult to make strong statements about user charges, to say unequivocally that they should generally be set either at zero or at full cost. The optimal mix of in-kind transfers and cash transfers and of targeting by income and by inability depends on considerations that vary widely among groups of recipients and among social services. As the social services expand and as policy-makers, designers, and economists learn about the behaviour of recipients, user-charge systems will continue to evolve.

APPENDIX A

Traditional models of cash and in-kind transfers

The standard proof for the general superiority of cash transfers over goods-specific subsidies is shown diagrammatically in Figure A.1.

In this general case, the consumer chooses between two commodities: the particular good being considered for subsidy and all other goods. In the diagram, S represents the particular good, and E represents income left over to purchase all other goods.

In the absence of any subsidy (cash or in kind), the consumer faces the budget line represented by *DAHF* and maximizes his utility at point A on indifference curve I_1.

If, however, good S is subsidized, the budget line shifts to *DMBG*, and the consumer maximizes his utility at point B on indifference curve I_2. The subsidy costs the government *BH*.

On the other hand, a cash transfer of KD = JH would present the consumer with budget line *KCJL* and result in his achieving the same indifference curve I_2 at point C. Since *JH* is less than *BH*, the cash transfer achieves the same result as the in-kind subsidy but at a lower cost.[1]

---

1 It must be pointed out that this proof involves partial equilibrium only, ignores taxation, and assumes that shifts in demand do not change prices and that the labour-leisure choice is not affected. Under certain assumptions (such as no other distortions and the possibility of lump-sum transfers), the theorem may also be demonstrated in a general equilibrium framework (see Friedman 1953, 100-13).

In the real world, of course, shifts in demand do alter prices, a subject that is dealt with in Chapters 3 and 4 and Appendices B and C. Tax revenues must be used to pay for any transfer system, as discussed in Appendices C, D, and F. Moreover, transfers may affect the leisure-labour choice, a subject discussed in Chapters 4 and 5. In such cases, the marginal tax on wages raises the cost to the consumer of purchasing a good (expressed in terms of foregone leisure) above the cost of producing it (expressed in terms of labour input). A goods-specific subsidy, financed by an income tax, reduces

118 Appendix A

Figure A.1
The general analysis of cash vs in-kind transfers.

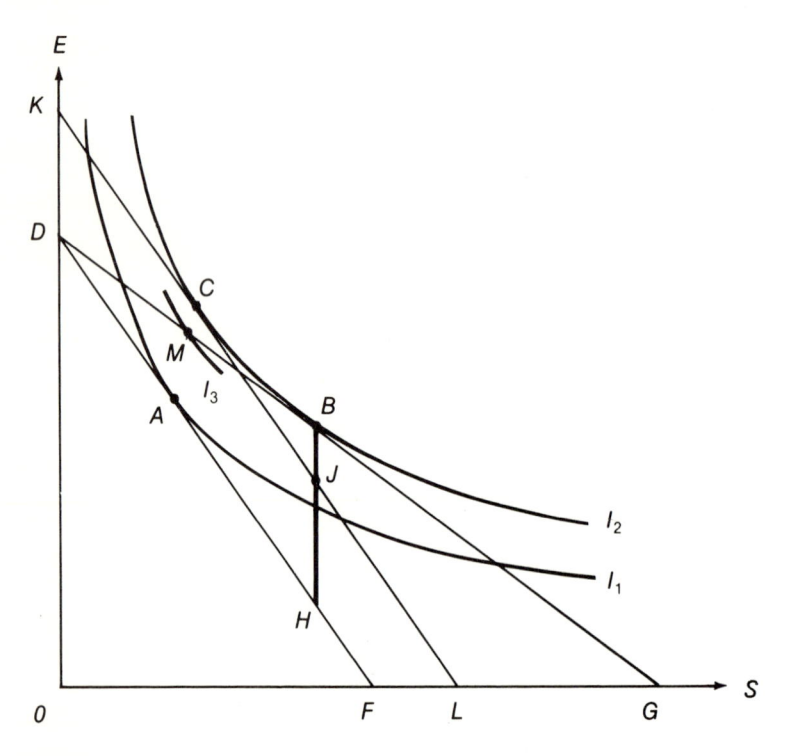

If the government uses the cash transfer, it saves that fraction of the subsidy represented by *BJ/BH*. Thus, the fraction may be seen as a measure of the relative inefficiency of the subsidy. It may be shown to increase with the elasticity of substitution between S and E.

---

this gap. The efficiency or inefficiency of the subsidy now depends on various elasticities of substitution in the recipient's utility function and, in the general case, on the characteristics of production. At this point, the problem becomes one of optimal taxation, for which there is an elaborate literature (see, for example, Baumol and Bradford 1970, and Diamond and Mirrlees 1971).

In a few cases, an optimal-taxation argument can be used to justify an in-kind transfer. For example, if a subsidy to day care induces a parent to enter the labour force, the resulting addition to tax revenue may justify a subsidy up to a maximum of tax deductibility (Krashinsky 1977, 69-81). It must be emphasized, however, that this approach can justify only limited subsidies to a few social services.

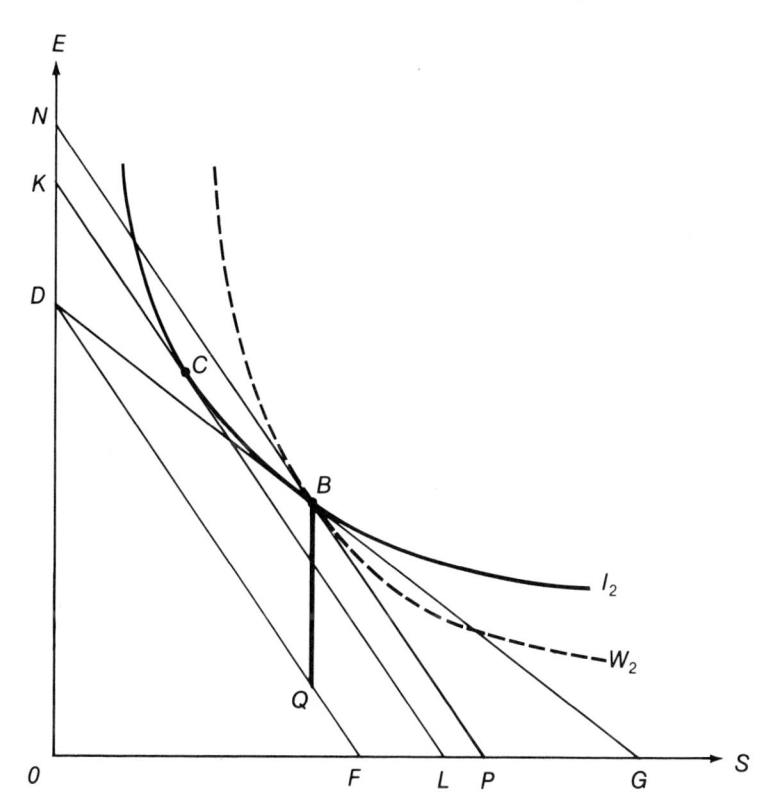

Figure A.2
Cash vs in-kind transfers for an incompetent recipient.

Note that the in-kind subsidy can become efficient if it is restricted to those consumers willing to consume the amount of good S available at point M, where the slope of indifference curve I_3 is the same as line KL. This amount, however, is likely to be so small as to be politically unattractive.

The situation changes dramatically if the values of society and the recipient differ so that we believe he is not as well off at point C as at point B. This situation, which involves incompetence or some other impairment of the utility function, is diagrammed in Figure A.2. Here, society believes that the indifference curve labelled W_2 runs through the true set of points at which the client is made equally well off, but the client, for some reason, prefers indifference curve I_2. In Figure A.2, line NBP shows the government's equal-cost alternatives.

Given cash, the incompetent client still chooses point C. Given a subsidy to good S, he chooses point B on budget line DBG to maximize his utility on indifference curve I_2. Since point B also maximizes the welfare of society on indifference curve W_2, it is the government's efficient choice, made for paternalistic reasons.

The subsidy for this situation is often presented as a minimum-purchase subsidy: the client is forced to purchase a minimum amount of S or lose the subsidy. This faces him with the budget line $DQBP$ (or $DQBG$) and induces him to purchase more S than he would if he were given free choice.

APPENDIX B

A simple model of overuse and inability

The issues of overuse and inability may be illustrated in a simple algebraic model.

If the individual's utility is dependent on his income, I, his inability, n, and the price of the need-good, P, we may write the indirect utility function V as

$$V = V(I, n, P). \tag{B.1}$$

If subsidization of the need-good is contemplated, then

$$P = P_0(1 - s) \tag{B.2}$$

where s is the rate of subsidy.

An increase in the subsidy rate increases the consumer's utility by

$$\frac{dV}{ds} = \frac{dV}{dP} \cdot \frac{dP}{ds}. \tag{B.3}$$

Now, using Roy's Theorem, with MU_I as the marginal utility of income and X as the quantity of the need-good to be consumed by the individual,

$$\frac{dV}{dP} = -MU_I X. \tag{B.4}$$

So equation (B.3) may be rewritten as

$$\frac{dV}{ds} = MU_I X P_0. \tag{B.5}$$

122 Appendix B

Now TC, the cost to the government of the subsidy, may be written as

$$TC = XP_0 s. \tag{B.6}$$

When the subsidy rate is increased, this cost rises by

$$\frac{dTC}{ds} = XP_0 + sP_0 \cdot \frac{dX}{ds} = XP_0 (1 + \frac{s}{X} \cdot \frac{dX}{ds}). \tag{B.7}$$

If E_D is the consumer's elasticity of demand for the need-good (where elasticity is written as a positive number), then

$$E_D = -\frac{P}{X} \cdot \frac{dX}{dP} = -\frac{P_0(1-s)}{X} \cdot \frac{dX}{(-P_0 ds)} = \frac{(1-s)}{X} \cdot \frac{dX}{ds}. \tag{B.8}$$

So equation (B.7) may be rewritten as

$$\frac{dTC}{ds} = XP_0 (1 + \frac{s}{1-s} E_D). \tag{B.9}$$

Thus, an additional cost of one dollar to the government is worth $1/(1 + [s/(1 - s)]E_D)$ to the recipient of the in-kind subsidy. When a lump-sum cash transfer occurs, however, one dollar in cost to the government is worth one dollar to the recipient (ignoring administration costs in both programs). Clearly, the in-kind subsidy is justified only if the marginal utility of income of the recipients exceeds that of the taxpayers *and* if it is not practical to use cash transfers to reach those in need.

It is also worth noting that the value of the in-kind program falls as E_D increases.

APPENDIX C

A model of inability and cash and in-kind transfers

The development of a model incorporating the theory of inability permits examination of both the usefulness of the concept and its effect on various issues involved in considering in-kind and cash transfers.

My model draws on the work of Munk (1977). There are, however, some basic differences. He explicitly allowed redistribution only by means of goods-specific programs priced below cost and financed by a general tax. My model explicitly presents a cash-transfer system as an alternative. It assumes that the programs do not affect labour supply; built into each program, however, is an efficiency-loss factor that might be interpreted as including any losses caused by changes in labour supply. (Some labour supply elasticity is built into the simulations presented in Appendix D.)

Assume that each consumer purchases only two goods. One is the need-good – the good that individuals with inability (as defined below) generally consume in larger-than-average amounts as part of the least-cost bundles they require to achieve what the government, acting for society, has set as the minimum standard of living. The other good in the model is a general commodity representing all other goods.

The consumer then combines these goods with leisure time and, depending on his endowment of various kinds of human capital (abilities, skills, health, and so on) and on his family circumstances (dependent parents, disabled children, the absence of a supportive extended family, and so on), produces various characteristics that enter his utility function. We may express the process that generates utility in the following three equations:

$$C_{Ei} = f(E_i, T_{Ei}, n_i), \tag{C.1}$$

$$C_{Xi} = g(X_i, T_{Xi}, n_i), \tag{C.2}$$

124 Appendix C

$$u_i = u(C_{Ei}, C_{Xi}),\tag{C.3}$$

where u_i is the utility of the ith consumer, X_i is his consumption of the need-good, E_i is his consumption of other goods, T_{Ei} and T_{Xi} are the time spent producing characteristics C_{Ei} and C_{Xi} respectively (those characteristics enter the utility function u), and n_i is a parameter representing the inability of the consumer. The value of n_i certainly affects the production of C_{Xi} and may affect the production of C_{Ei} (higher values of n_i reduce production). The household production functions are represented by f and g.

This functional form suggests the definition of inability used in the text: any condition or situation that reduces the characteristics that the consumer can produce from a given set of inputs. To put it another way, inability increases the inputs a consumer requires to produce a given set of characteristics. For the welfare programs this book is concerned with, inability increases the inputs (more precisely, the cost of the inputs) a client requires to produce the set of characteristics consistent with the minimum level of well-being implied by the poverty line.

Since this model is not concerned with the details of household production, we may write the consumer's utility function in the standard way, keeping the intermediate production process in mind. Thus

$$u_i = u(E_i, X_i, T_i, n_i),\tag{C.4}$$

where T_i is total leisure time (equal to $T_{Ei} + T_{Xi}$). The price of E_i is set at one, so that E_i may be interpreted as income available for other goods.

The consumer is assumed not to adjust his supply of labour, so his income before taxes is fixed at Y_i. The government may subsidize the need-good and may operate a cash-transfer program; it pays for these programs by a general income tax. The consumer's budget constraint is thus

$$E_i + p(1 - s)X_i = Y_i - \theta(Y_i, \tau) + \phi(Y_i, \mu).\tag{C.5}$$

The full cost of the need good is represented by p (the good is assumed to be in perfectly elastic supply), and s is the subsidy towards the purchase of the good. The income tax is represented by $\theta_i = \theta(Y_i, \tau)$ and depends only on the consumer's income and on the general level of the tax, represented by τ (so that, by definition, $\Sigma \theta(Y_i, \tau) = \tau$). The cash transfer received by the consumer is represented by $\phi_i = \phi(Y_i, \mu)$; it depends only on the consumer's income and on the general level of the transfer program, represented by μ (so that, by definition, $\Sigma \phi(Y_i, \mu) = \mu$). (Of course, for certain values of τ and μ, some consumers pay no tax and some receive no transfers, although all may receive the subsidy.)

A model of inability 125

If each consumer maximizes utility subject to this budget constraint, then his utility may be written indirectly (represented by v_i) as a function of the price of X, where $P = p(1 - s)$, before-tax income, and the levels of the tax and transfer. Thus,

$$v_i = v_i(P, Y_i, \tau, \mu), \tag{C.6}$$

remembering that the function v_i varies among consumers according to n_i, which is set by their endowments of qualities, such as health, disability, education, and intelligence, and by their family circumstances.

Of course, each program has some losses associated with it. For each $(1 + k_\tau)$ dollars the consumer pays in taxes, the government receives only one dollar in revenue. For each dollar in transfers the consumer receives, the government must pay out $(1 + k_\mu)$ dollars. Each dollar consumers receive in the subsidy program costs the government $(1 + k_s)$ dollars. If X is total consumption of the need good (so that $X = \Sigma X_i$), then total government revenue R may be written as

$$R = \tau/(1 + k_\tau) - (1 + k_\mu)\mu - (1 + k_s)psX. \tag{C.7}$$

Assume that the government is constrained by other policies to keep R constant. The problem then is to set s, μ, and τ so as to maximize some social welfare function W, keeping R constant. If we assume that the social welfare function is additive, so that

$$W = \sum_i v_i(P, Y_i, \tau, \mu), \tag{C.8}$$

the problem becomes a straightforward exercise in maximization. The Lagrangian is

$$L = \sum_i v_i - \delta[\overline{R} - \tau/(1 + k_\tau) + (1 + k_\mu)\mu + (1 + k_s)psX]. \tag{C.9}$$

Differentiating,

$$\partial L/\partial s = \sum_i(-p\partial v_i/\partial P) - \delta[(1 + k_s)p(X + s\partial X/\partial s)]; \tag{C.10}$$

$$\partial L/\partial \tau = \sum_i(\partial v_i/\partial \tau) - \delta[(1 + k_s)ps\partial X/\partial \tau - 1/(1 + k_\tau)]; \tag{C.11}$$

$$\partial L/\partial \mu = \sum_i(\partial v_i/\partial \mu) - \delta[(1 + k_s)ps\partial X/\partial \mu + (1 + k_\mu)]. \tag{C.12}$$

Note, however, that assuming a fixed labour supply has eliminated a number of potential terms in these expressions. Unfortunately, this means that any losses

126 Appendix C

in efficiency that might occur because of reactions in the labour supply end up buried in k_s, k_τ, and k_μ.

The conditions for a maximum are obtained by setting expressions (C.10) (C.11), and (C.12) equal to zero. It is also useful to observe that, using Roy's Theorem,

$$\partial v_i/\partial P = -\lambda_i X_i, \qquad (C.13)$$

$$\partial v_i/\partial \tau = -\lambda_i \partial \theta_i/\partial \tau, \qquad (C.14)$$

$$\partial v_i/\partial \mu = \lambda_i \partial \phi_i/\partial \mu, \qquad (C.15)$$

where λ_i is the marginal utility of income of the ith consumer.[1] Combining these three equations with equations (C.10), (C.11), and (C.12) set equal to zero yields

$$\frac{\sum_i (\lambda_i X_i)}{(1+k_s)(X+s\partial X/\partial s)} = \frac{\sum_i (\lambda_i \partial \theta_i/\partial \tau)}{1/(1+k_\tau) - (1+k_s)ps\partial X/\partial \tau}$$

$$= \frac{\sum_i (\lambda_i \partial \phi_i/\partial \mu)}{(1+k_\mu) + (1+k_s)ps\partial X/\partial \mu}. \qquad (C.16)$$

Let us now follow Munk in defining Z_s, the distributional characteristic of the subsidy, Z_τ, the distributional characteristic of the tax, and Z_μ, the distributional characteristic of the cash transfer:

$$Z_s = \sum_i (\lambda_i X_i/X), \qquad (C.17)$$

$$Z_\tau = \sum_i (\lambda_i \partial \theta_i/\partial \tau), \qquad (C.18)$$

$$Z_\mu = \sum_i (\lambda_i \partial \phi_i/\partial \mu). \qquad (C.19)$$

Z_s, Z_τ, and Z_μ are the weighted averages of the marginal utilities of income, where the weights are, respectively, the relative consumption of the need good,

---

1 If the social welfare function is not simply additive, the λ_i would be equal to $(\partial W/\partial v_i)$ $(\partial v_i/\partial Y_i^d)$, where Y^d is the disposable income of the ith household. Thus λ_i would be the marginal social welfare of an increase in the ith family's income.

the portion of a tax increase that is borne by the household, and the portion of transfer increase that accrues to the household.

It is also useful to define E_D, the price elasticity of demand for the need good, and to note that

$$E_D = -(\partial X/\partial P)(P/X) = (\partial X/\partial s)(1-s)/X. \tag{C.20}$$

By applying equations (C.17), (C.18), (C.19), and (C.20) to the equations in (C.16), the following equilibrium conditions can be derived:

$$\frac{Z_\mu}{Z_\tau} = \frac{(1+k_\mu) + (1+k_s)ps\partial X/\partial \mu}{1/(1+k_\tau) - (1+k_s)ps\partial X/\partial \tau}; \tag{C.21}$$

$$\frac{Z_\mu}{Z_s} = \frac{(1+k_\mu)/(1+k_s) + ps\partial X/\partial \mu}{1 + E_D s/(1-s)}. \tag{C.22}$$

Equation (C.21) states simply that redistribution via the transfer program should continue as long as the gains to recipients exceed the losses to taxpayers. (This statement will become clearer when this equation is simplified below.)

This redistribution having been achieved, equation (C.22) provides an implicit solution for the subsidy rate s. Consider the right-hand side of the equation. This expression is a function of s that has the value $(1 + k_\mu)/(1 + k_s)$ when $s = 0$ and whose value decreases to zero when s increases to one (although the expression need not decrease monotonically unless $ps\partial X/\partial \mu$ is much less than one, an assumption to be defended later). Thus a necessary and sufficient condition for $s > 0$ is that $(1 + k_\mu)/(1 + k_s) > Z_\mu/Z_s$.

Written another way, this condition states that $s > 0$ if and only if $Z_s/(1 + k_s) > Z_\mu/(1 + k_\mu)$. In other words, the need-good X should be subsidized only if $1/(1 + k_s)$ dollars spent on the subsidy increases the utility of recipients more than $1/(1 + k_\mu)$ dollars spent on the cash-transfer program. This condition and the solution for s are shown diagrammatically in Figure C.1.

Equation (C.22) also permits the demonstration of the existence of a unique, optimal s. Define a function $f(s)$ equal to the right-hand side of equation (C.22):

$$f(s) = \frac{(1+k_\mu)/(1+k_s) + ps\partial X/\partial \mu}{1 + E_D s/(1-s)} \tag{C.23}$$

Clearly $f(0) = (1 + k_\mu)/(1 + k_s)$, while $f(1) = 0$, so that equation (C.22), which may be rewritten as

128 Appendix C

Figure C.1
A diagrammatic solution for s. See equation (C.23).

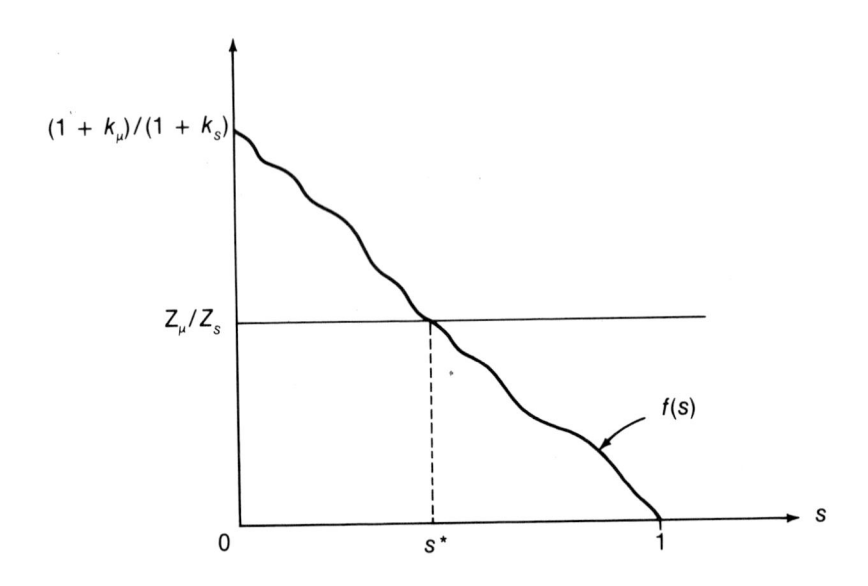

$$f(s) = Z_\mu/Z_s, \qquad (C.24)$$

must have a solution on the unit interval if f is continuous on the unit interval and if $(1 + k_\mu)/(1 + k_s) > Z_\mu/Z_s$. (This is clear from Figure C.1.) Only if $f(s)$ is monotonic downward is this sufficient condition also necessary. Furthermore, if $f(s)$ is monotonic downward, any solution to equation (C.22) must be unique. Differentiating equation (C.23), it may be shown that

$$f'(s) = \frac{df}{ds} = \frac{-E_D(1 + k_\mu)/(1 + k_s) + [(1-s)^2 - E_D s^2]p\partial X/\partial \mu}{[1 + E_D s/(1-s)]^2 (1-s)^2}. \qquad (C.25)$$

Clearly $f(s)$ is monotonic downward if $f'(s)$ is negative everywhere on the unit interval. This occurs if

$$\frac{(1+k_\mu)E_D}{(1+k_s)p\partial X/\partial\mu} > (1-s)^2 - E_D s^2 \tag{C.26}$$

for all s in the unit interval. Now the right-hand side of equation (C.26) is a quadratic function of s (call the function g) that attains its maximum value on the unit interval [0, 1] at $s = 0$, where $g(0) = 1$. Thus, $f(s)$ is monotonic downward if

$$\frac{(1+k_\mu)E_D}{(1+k_s)p\partial X/\partial\mu} > 1, \tag{C.27}$$

or if

$$\frac{(1+k_\mu)}{(1+k_s)p\partial X/\partial\mu} > 1/E_D \tag{C.28}$$

If $p\partial X/\partial\mu$ is very small (much less than one, but positive), then this condition holds unless E_D is very large (in which case the value of s is quite small, if not zero).

Let us now return to the explicit consideration of cash and in-kind transfer programs. Assume first that $k_s = k_\mu$ (that is, that the subsidy and the cash-transfer programs are equally effective at transmitting one dollar of the taxpayers' money to recipients). In this case, the condition for a positive subsidy ($s > 0$) is that Z_s be greater than Z_μ. In other words, individuals who would benefit by the subsidy must have higher marginal utilities of income (that is, be lower down the utility distribution scale) than those who would benefit from the cash-transfer program. In order for this to occur, two conditions must hold: first, inability must vary significantly so that those who require the good generally have low utilities; second, those who need the good must not be easily identifiable for cash transfers. Notice that if the needy can be easily identified for cash transfers, then Z_s equals Z_μ, no matter how extreme their inability, and no subsidy is justified.

It should also be noted that when a subsidy is justified, its optimal value becomes larger with increasing inelasticity of the demand for X. However, even if E_D is close to zero, the subsidy is still limited, because as s rises, the recipients are made better off, which raises their utilities, lowers their marginal utilities of income, and hence lowers Z_s.

The argument for a subsidy is made stronger (and the optimal value of s, the subsidy rate, is increased) if k_s is less than k_μ. At first glance, this may appear to

130 Appendix C

be unlikely, since administration costs are likely to be higher in an in-kind program. However, k_μ and k_s may also include efficiency losses caused by the programs' negative effect on labour supply. (These effects are suppressed in the model.) Unless the good X is a particularly strong substitute or complement for leisure, there is no reason why equivalent in-kind and cash transfer should have different effects on the labour supply, assuming that both programs reduce their benefits in the same manner as income rises. However, cash transfers and in-kind programs are generally directed to different groups of consumers. Cash transfers may reach all the poor, but in-kind transfers reach only a particular subgroup that is in need. If this subgroup has a different labour supply curve, then k_s may well be less than k_μ. This is particularly likely to occur if the subgroup is such that its supply of labour is not affected by transfers (for example, if it consists of the old or retarded) or if the in-kind transfer in question can increase this subgroup's labour supply (for example, if the subsidized program assists disabled individuals to re-enter society and work or provides single parents with day care so they may enter the labour market).[2]

An explicit solution for s in the model may be obtained by making a simplifying assumption following Munk. Assume that when the level of taxation is increased, the increase's direct effect on the government deficit dominates the effect on the deficit through any income effect on the consumption of X (that is, that $ps\partial X/\partial \tau$ is much less than one). Similarly, assume that when the level of transfers is increased, the direct effect on the deficit through μ dominates the effect through any increase of X (that is, that $ps\partial X/\partial \mu$ is much less than one.)

The model then solves to

$$Z_\mu/Z_\tau = (1 + k_\tau)(1 + k_\mu); \tag{C.29}$$

$$\frac{s}{1-s} = \frac{1}{E_D}\left(\frac{Z_s(1+k_\mu)}{Z_\mu(1+k_s)} - 1\right). \tag{C.30}$$

In equation (C.29), income redistribution clearly depends on each dollar of a cash transfer giving recipients a gain that exceeds the taxpayers' losses in providing it. In other words, a dollar in taxes received by the government costs taxpayers $(1 + k_\tau)$ dollars, where k_τ includes administration costs and efficiency losses caused by any elasticity of labour supply; each dollar spent by the government generates $1/(1 + k_\mu)$ in value to recipients, where again k_μ includes administration costs and efficiency losses. This can be seen by rewriting equation (C.29) as

---

2 For a discussion of this point with regard to day care, see Krashinsky (1977, 57-81).

A model of inability 131

$$Z_\mu/(1+k_\mu) = (1+k_\tau)Z_\tau. \tag{C.31}$$

Now, in equation (C.30), the existence of the subsidy again clearly depends on $Z_s/(1+k_s)$ being larger than $Z_\mu/(1+k_\mu)$. The size of the subsidy again clearly depends on E_D, the elasticity of demand for the subsidized good.

The reader may observe that equations (C.21) and (C.22) represent only two of three possible equations coming out of equation (C.16). The third, which is not independent of equations (C.21) and (C.22), is

$$\frac{Z_\tau}{Z_s} = \frac{1/[(1+k_\tau)(1+k_s)] - ps\partial X/\partial \tau}{1 + E_D s/(1-s)}. \tag{C.32}$$

Again, assuming that $ps\partial X/\partial \tau$ is much less than one, an explicit solution for s may be obtained:

$$\frac{s}{1-s} = \frac{1}{E_D}\left(\frac{Z_s}{Z_\tau(1+k_\tau)(1+k_s)} - 1\right). \tag{C.33}$$

Basically, equation (C.33) states that the in-kind program is desirable when the value of one dollar paid in a subsidy to the recipient is greater than the value lost by taxpayers in providing that dollar. Note that providing one dollar in benefits costs taxpayers $(1+k_\tau)(1+k_s)$ because of both administration costs and efficiency losses caused by shifts in the supply of labour.

If income redistribution through cash transfers were not possible, equation (C.33) would dictate the optimal pattern of price subsidies to help the poor. However, since cash transfers are the backbone of any redistributional strategy, equation (C.29) suggests that they should be used to raise the welfare (and hence to lower the average marginal utility of income) of any easily (that is, cheaply) identifiable group in need. Where the group is not easily identified because of the moral-hazard problems discussed in Chapters 3 and 4, in-kind subsidies may be efficient if the principal users of the subsidized commodity are persons in need, in other words if Z_s is large, relative to Z_τ and Z_μ, after redistribution by cash transfers.

Note that redistribution in this model requires that persons in need (that is, those with low utilities) have high marginal utilities of income so that before redistribution by cash transfers, Z_μ is much greater than Z_τ, and even after cash transfers, Z_s remains larger than both Z_μ and Z_τ. Ignoring inability, this requirement is satisfied by assuming that all consumers have identical utility functions (at least as a function of income) and that the marginal utility of income falls as income rises. Introducing inability raises a problem: an increase in inability reduces utility, but there is no *a priori* reason why it may not also reduce the marginal utility of income. For example, a person who requires very expensive medical care has low utility, but the high cost of assisting him makes the utility of one extra dollar of income also quite low.

One response to this problem is to argue that many inabilities do not alter the relationship between utility and the marginal utility of income; they only reduce utility. In these cases, inability creates additional needs and lowers the individual's utility relative to able people with the same income. If the inable person receives additional income and/or goods to compensate for his additional need, he then has the same income *and* the same marginal utility of income as those others. His consumption pattern may differ from that of others, but this difference is not seen as significant for public policy. Treating inability in this manner (that is, as equivalent to a loss of income) is, to some extent, an ethical approach. When inability is not extreme, equity suggests that need caused by inability should be treated similarly to need caused by low income.

In extreme cases, however, this response is not valid. For example, persons who are gravely disabled or have serious (and expensive) illnesses may not be viewed as having marginal utilities of income as high as other poor individuals. In these cases, the goal of maximizing an additive social welfare function is at odds with the notion of horizontal equity. This does not mean that these people can receive no assistance in this model. It is possible to use a more general social welfare function, one that is not additive but that places additional weight on raising the utilities of those below some standard of living.[3] It would result in establishing programs to raise all individuals above the poverty line (defined in terms of utility) with restrictions on further transfers to those whose marginal utilities of income are relatively low. It must be noted, however, that this course violates the principle of horizontal equity.[4]

Finally, the reader should observe that although, throughout the discussion, the subsidy *s* has appeared to be available to all consumers, there is nothing in

---

3 Thus W would be defined as $W = W(v_1, v_2, \ldots)$, and this would alter the definition of λ_i to that suggested in footnote 1: $\lambda_i = (\partial W/\partial v_i)(\partial v_i/\partial Y_i^d)$. No matter how low the marginal utility of income, $\partial W/\partial v_i$ (and hence λ_i) would be very large so long as v_i is below some minimum standard of living.

4 For example, a greatly disabled person who requires very expensive care might not receive funds beyond those necessary to achieve a minimum standard of living. Even this arrangement is not obvious: if that care is expensive enough, is it always appropriate to help that person at the expense of many others who could use the resources? So far, the response has been yes, but as medical techniques for extending life become ever more available at ever increasing cost (per unit of time extended), this question will become more difficult in a publicly funded system of insurance.

the model to prevent restricting it to those who can qualify under tests of inability (usually these tests use very rough measures) and/or income. Even without such tests, use of the subsidy may be self-limiting; many subsidized commodities are not usually purchased by persons without some level of inability. (Medical care, for example, is generally not purchased in large quantities by those who are not ill.) The general impact on the model of such limits is to raise Z_s and hence increase the case for the subsidy. (These and other limits are discussed in Chapter 4 and Appendix F.)

APPENDIX D

Computer simulations of inability and optimal subsidies

The model developed in Appendix C shows that unique values can exist for subsidies for a need-good X, a commodity used disproportionately by persons suffering from inability. It is useful to examine some numerical solutions for the subsidy rate to see what happens to it when various parameters are changed.

Two computer simulations were run assuming specific utility functions for specific groups of consumers and computing values that would maximize social welfare. Both programs assumed that all consumers (with or without inability) use the commodity in question, wealthier consumers use more of it, and all consumers increase their consumption of it when its price falls. However, if an individual suffers from inability of an undefined form, then, other things constant, he consumes more of the need-good. Assuming that this inability cannot be measured for purposes of adjusting a cash transfer, then the simulations, like the algebraic model, demonstrate that under certain circumstances (certain values of the parameters), it is desirable to subsidize the need-good.

The simulations employ a nested CES utility function shown below in equation (D.1): a, b, c, d, and e are parameters set equal for all consumers, n_i measures the individual's inability, X_i is the quantity consumed of the commodity being considered for subsidy, E_i is income available to purchase other goods, T_i is leisure time consumed, T_0 is total time available, P is the market price of the good being considered for subsidy, s is the subsidy rate, and h is a function relating disposable income to earned income. Earned income before taxes or transfers equals $(T_0 - T_i)W_i$.

Each consumer maximizes his utility function,

$$u_i = [c\{a(X_i - n_i)^{-b} + (1-a)E_i^{-b}\}^{d/b} + (1-c)T_i^{-d}]^{-e/d}, \qquad (D.1)$$

subject to the income constraint,

TABLE D.1

Consumers in the simulations

i	NUM_i	W_i	N_i
1	3	2	0
2	1	2	2000
3	1	2	4000
4	15	4	0
5	5	4	2000
6	5	4	4000
7	18	6	0
8	6	6	2000
9	6	6	4000
10	18	8	0
11	6	8	2000
12	6	8	4000
13	6	12	0
14	2	12	2000
15	2	12	4000

$$P(1-s)X_i + E_i = h(T_0 w_i - T_i W_i). \tag{D.2}$$

Both simulations use 100 consumers divided into fifteen categories, as shown in Table D.1. NUM_i is the number of consumers in each category, and N_i is a variable to be used in defining inability. The values of NUM_i and W_i are chosen so that if all consumers work 2000 hours, the distribution of earned income resembles that in Canada in 1977. N_i is set and distributed arbitrarily to demonstrate the point about inability, and $n_i = (\text{NEED})N_i$ so that the parameter NEED describes the spread of inability among consumers.

The constants b and d are defined so as to set the elasticity of substitution of E for X equal to the parameter ESUBEX and the elasticity of substitution of goods for time equal to the parameter ESUBGT. The constants a and c are defined so that when there is no subsidy (when $s = 0$ and $t = 0.5$), the seventh consumer ($W_7 = 6, N_7 = 0$) chooses the ratio of X to E and the ratio of T to E equal to the parameters XER and TER respectively. This is done by defining the following variables:

$$b = (1 - \text{ESUBEX})/\text{ESUBEX}, \tag{D.3}$$

$$d = (1 - \text{ESUBGT})/\text{ESUBGT}, \tag{D.4}$$

$$a = (\text{XER})^{b+1}/[1 + (\text{XER})^{b+1}], \tag{D.5}$$

136 Appendix D

$$y = (\text{TER})^{-1-d}/[3(1-a)(a\text{XER}^{-b} + 1-a)^{-1+d/b}], \qquad (D.6)$$

$$c = y/(1+y). \qquad (D.7)$$

The constant e represents the degree of the function. If e is set at 0.5, then doubling $X_i - n_i$, E_i, and T_i increases u_i by the square root of 2. In technical terms, the utility function is homogeneous of degree e in E_i, T_i, and $(X_i - n_i)$. Finally, in the simulations, $P = 1$ and $T_0 = 6000$.

The simulations shown in this appendix differ only in their definition of h, which is a function that acts like a negative income tax. In the first simulation, the minimum guaranteed income is held fixed; in the second, it is allowed to vary.

In the first simulation, h is defined as

$$h(T_0 w_i - T_i w_i) = (T_0 - T_i) w_i (1 - t) + G(2 - 2t), \qquad (D.8)$$

where t is the tax rate on earning and G is government transfers when earnings are zero and t is set at 0.5. (The particular form of equation (D.8) will be explained later.) The value of G is held constant; s and t are varied so as to maximize social welfare (defined, as in equation (C.8), as the sum of individual utilities), subject to the constraint that government revenue not change. The optimal value of s is computed for various values of the parameters.

In the second simulation, the function h is defined slightly differently – and more naturally – as

$$h(T_0 w_i - T_i w_i) = (T_0 - T_i) w_i (1 - t) + G. \qquad (D.9)$$

Now G, s, and t are all allowed to vary so as to maximize social welfare, still subject to the constraint that government revenue not vary. Again, the optimal value of s is computed for various values of the parameters.

The results of the two simulations are interesting both in their similarities and in their differences.

SIMULATION HOLDING G (minimum guaranteed income) FIXED

In the first simulation, initially t is set at 0.5, and s at zero. The consumers maximize utility, and their decisions about labour supply generate tax revenue of TR1:

$$\text{TR}1 = \sum_i (\text{NUM}_i) t (T_0 - T_i). \qquad (D.10)$$

The values of utility are added up to generate SUMU, assumed to be the social welfare function. If s is set at any value greater than zero, and if t is raised above 0.5, then consumers' new decisions about T_i, X_i, and E_i generate a new level of net revenue TR2 for the government:

$$\text{TR}2 = \sum_i (\text{NUM}_i)[t(T_0 - T_i) + 2tG - sPX_i]. \tag{D.11}$$

Now the lowest value of t is chosen that sets TR2 = TR1. (If no such such value of t exists, then an inappropriate choice for s has been made.) The computer simulation next examines the various possible values of s (each time choosing t to generate the same net revenue) and picks the s that maximizes SUMU, the social welfare function.

The particular form of the budget constraint – equation (D.8) – can now be explained. When a subsidy is financed by a rise in taxes, that rise falls proportionately on earned income $(T_0 - T_i)w_i$ and on the government transfer G. For example, when $t = 0.5$, the right side of equation (D.8) is $0.5(T_0 - T_i)w_i + G$, but when $t = 0.6$, the right side becomes $0.4(T_0 - T_i)w_i + 0.8G$. Therefore, the rise in taxes appears to fall proportionately on all income groups, whatever proportion of their income is earned. Thus, this somewhat unnatural form for the budget restraint demonstrates that a subsidy may be justified even when it is subsidized by a proportional tax and when the income elasticity of the demand for the good is unitary, so that the program does not generally redistribute income from those with high incomes to those with lower incomes. The detailed breakdown in Table D.4 shows that redistribution actually occurs *within* each income class, and that it goes from those of low need to those of high need.

If need is sufficiently varied, the subsidy raises social welfare even though it also generates two inefficiencies: overconsumption of the need-good (because of the subsidy) and undersupply of labour (because of the rise of the tax rate on earnings). In general, overconsumption of X falls with the price elasticity of demand for X. This elasticity is related to ESUBEX, the elasticity of substitution between E_i and X_i. The lower is ESUBEX, the less responsive is the ratio X_i/E_i to changes in relative prices induced by the subsidy.

The second inefficiency, undersupply of labour, falls with the labour supply elasticity, which is related to ESUBGT, the elasticity of substitution between goods and time. The lower is ESUBGT, the less responsive is the ratio $[a(X_i - n_i)^{-b} + (1 - a)E_i^{-b}]/T_i$ to changes in relative prices induced by the change in taxes.

Figures D.1, D.2, and D.3 show the optimal value of s for various values of ESUBEX, ESUBGT, and NEED, the variation in inability among consumers. (The

138 Appendix D

Figure D.1
Optimal values of s for various values of ESUBEX and ESUBGT when NEED = 1.0. XER = TER = e = 0.5. All lines represent an approximate fit of the points obtained in the simulation.

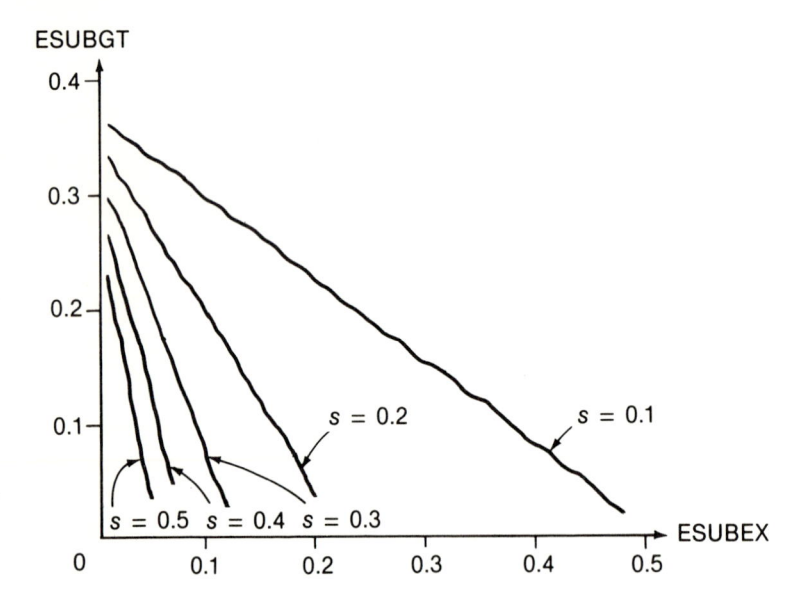

optimal value of s is the subsidy financed by an equal revenue increase in t that maximizes SUMU). In the graphs, e, XER, and TER are all set at 0.5. It is clear that a reduction in either ESUBEX or ESUBGT increases s and that when ESUBEX and ESUBGT are quite small, the value of s can be significant.

Table D.2 shows that an increase in NEED increases the optimal value of s. Table D.3 shows that a decrease in e that increases the marginal utility of income of the poor and needy relative to the rich (and hence increases the benefits to redistribution) also increases the optimal value of s. Even when $e = 1, s > 0$. This occurs because the utility function is then homogeneous of degree one in T_i, E_i, and $(X_i - n_i)$, so a higher level of inability gives a consumer a higher marginal utility of income. Thus, a subsidy that redistributes income towards the needy may also redistribute utility.

A closer look at some of the simulated consumers suggests the way in which this model redistributes income. Table D.4 shows the utility of one consumer from each of the fifteen groups when $s = 0$ and again when s is set at its optimal

Simulations of inability and optimal subsidies 139

Figure D.2
Optimal values of s for various values of ESUBEX and ESUBGT when NEED = 1.4. XER = TER = e = 0.5. All lines represent an approximate fit of the points obtained in the simulation.

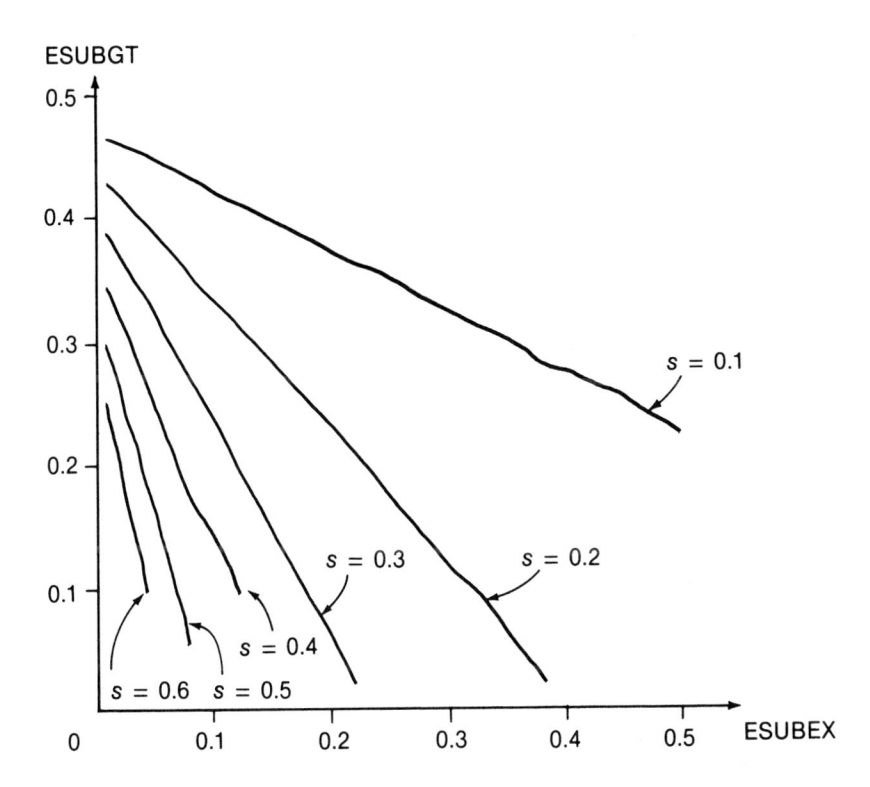

value. In all these cases, the values of e, TER, and XER are set at 0.5, while ESUBEX and ESUBGT are set at 0.1; NEED varies from 0.5 up to 2.0.

Table D.4 shows clearly that redistribution from high-income to low-income consumers may not be appropriate, since it would not necessarily assist those who have both high income and high inability (for example, consumers 9 and 12). On the other hand, the subsidy, financed by a tax that affects all consumers proportionately, effectively redistributes from those with no inability to those with high inability, whatever their income. Within each income class, for each

Figure D.3
Optimal values of s for various values of ESUBEX and ESUBGT when NEED = 2.0. XER = TER = e = 0.5. All lines represent an approximate fit of the points obtained in the simulation.

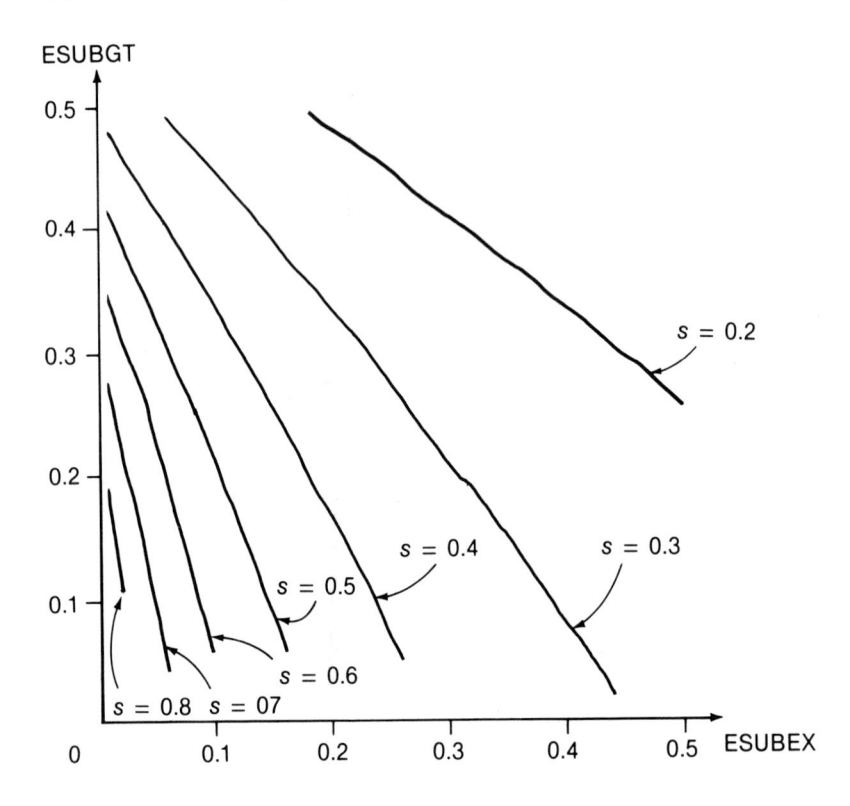

value of NEED, utility is 'redistributed' from consumers with N_i = 0 to consumers with N_i = 4000. The larger is NEED, the more significant is the effect on SUMU, the total utility.

SIMULATION ALLOWING G TO VARY

In the second simulation, G is allowed to vary, and the values of s, G, and t are to be chosen to maximize SUMU while holding government revenue constant. The budget constraint facing the individual consumer is changed to

TABLE D.2

Optimal values of s as need rises

		SUMU	
NEED	Optimal s	When $s = 0$	When s = optimal s
0.0	0.004	8309.16	8309.16
0.1	0.038	8285.93	8285.94
0.2	0.078	8262.49	8262.54
0.3	0.128	8238.84	8238.99
0.4	0.181	8214.97	8215.30
0.5	0.231	8190.86	8191.49
0.6	0.289	8166.52	8167.58
0.7	0.336	8141.93	8143.59
0.8	0.388	8117.08	8119.53
0.9	0.434	8091.95	8095.41
1.0	0.477	8066.55	8071.24
1.1	0.512	8040.85	8047.03
1.2	0.546	8014.84	8022.79
1.3	0.578	7988.50	7998.50
1.4	0.605	7961.81	7974.19
1.5	0.630	7934.75	7949.84
1.6	0.653	7907.29	7925.46
1.7	0.673	7879.40	7901.05
1.8	0.693	7851.06	7876.61
1.9	0.709	7822.17	7852.13
2.0	0.727	7792.72	7827.62
2.1	0.742	7762.58	7803.08
2.2	0.756	7731.63	7778.50
2.3	0.768	7699.57	7753.88
2.4	0.780	7665.75	7729.23

NOTE: e = XER = TER = 0.5, ESUBEX = 0.05, ESUBGT = 0.05

$$P(1 - s)X_i + E_i = (T_0 - T_i)w_i(1 - t) + G. \tag{D.9}$$

Since G, the cash guarantee level, is allowed to vary, there is no point in linking it to t as in equation (D.8).

Initially, G is set at 4000, t at 0.5, and s at 0, and a value of TR1 is generated as in the first simulation (so that the results of the two simulations can be compared directly). Since G is to vary, TR1 is defined to include all cash transfers:

$$\text{TR}1 = -100G + \sum_i (\text{NUM}_i) t(T_0 - T_i). \tag{D.12}$$

TABLE D.3

Optimal values of s as e varies

e	Optimal s
0.1	0.576
0.2	0.556
0.3	0.532
0.4	0.508
0.5	0.477
0.6	0.438
0.7	0.395
0.8	0.336
0.9	0.273
1.0	0.193

NOTE: See note to Table D.2.

For each set of values of G, t, and s, government revenue may be expressed as

$$\text{TR}2 = -100G + \sum_i (\text{NUM}_i)[t(T_0 - T_i) - sPX_i]. \tag{D.13}$$

If TR2 is constrained to be equal to TR1, optimal values of s and G (and hence t) can be obtained so as to maximize SUMU.

Figures D.4 and D.5 show the results for the optimal value of s for various values of ESUBEX, ESUBGT, and NEED, holding e, XER, and TER all equal to 0.5. The values for NEED are set at 1.0 and 1.4, so the two figures can be compared with Figures D.1 and D.2. (Computational complexities made computations for NEED = 2.0 impractical.) Although the shapes of the curves have changed, the qualitative result has not. The optimal subsidy is significant for reasonable values of the elasticity. Furthermore, unlike the situation in Figures D.1 and D.2, even if ESUBGT is relatively high, the optimal subsidy is still significant so long as ESUBEX is very small. A low value of ESUBEX suggests that consumers find additional units of X_i (beyond their need) to have rapidly diminishing value. This is fundamentally the case for in-kind transfers. If moral-hazard problems make it expensive to identify the needy for cash transfers, it may be more efficient to allow consumers to self-select according to inability by subsidizing the good in the marketplace. Such self-selection is efficient only if more able consumers do not overuse the good in question because it is subsidized. A low value of ESUBEX ensures that overuse does not take place.

Table D.5 (which should be compared to Table D.4) shows what happens to the utility distribution by illustrating the effects of allowing G to vary. For each of three values of NEED, the first column shows each consumer's utility when

TABLE D.4

Values of utility when $s = 0$ and $s =$ optimal value

Consumer	NEED = 0.5 $s=0$ $t=0.5$	NEED = 0.5 $s=0.1035$ $t=0.5190$	NEED = 1.0 $s=0$ $t=0.5$	NEED = 1.0 $s=0.2827$ $t=0.5580$	NEED = 1.4 $s=0$ $t=0.5$	NEED = 1.4 $s=0.4189$ $t=0.5920$	NEED = 2.0 $s=0$ $t=0.5$	NEED = 2.0 $s=0.5742$ $t=0.6380$
1 ($W=2, N=0$)	66.98	66.88	66.98	66.43	66.98	65.78	66.98	64.49
2 ($W=2, N=2000$)	63.54	63.69	59.91	60.80	56.84	58.86	51.88	56.41
3 ($W=2, N=4000$)	59.91	60.33	51.88	54.60	44.43	51.01	29.95	46.95
4 ($W=4, N=0$)	75.36	75.27	75.36	74.85	75.36	74.25	75.36	73.06
5 ($W=4, N=2000$)	72.96	73.04	70.49	70.95	68.45	69.48	65.26	67.48
6 ($W=4, N=4000$)	70.49	70.75	65.26	66.83	60.75	64.34	53.28	61.40
7 ($W=6, N=0$)	80.58	80.50	80.58	80.12	80.58	79.58	80.58	78.49
8 ($W=6, N=2000$)	78.73	78.78	76.83	77.11	75.28	75.89	72.89	74.18
9 ($W=6, N=4000$)	76.83	77.02	72.89	73.98	69.57	72.01	64.28	69.60
10 ($W=8, N=0$)	84.21	84.14	84.21	83.79	84.21	83.29	84.21	82.29
11 ($W=8, N=2000$)	82.69	82.72	81.15	81.33	79.89	80.28	77.96	78.77
12 ($W=8, N=4000$)	81.15	81.29	77.96	78.79	75.32	77.14	71.17	75.07
13 ($W=12, N=0$)	88.97	88.91	88.97	88.62	88.97	88.20	88.97	87.34
14 ($W=12, N=2000$)	87.85	87.87	86.72	86.80	85.80	85.97	84.41	84.74
15 ($W=12, N=4000$)	86.72	86.81	84.41	84.95	82.51	83.69	79.58	82.05
SUMU	7937.54	7937.73	7817.06	7819.16	7715.54	7722.24	7551.65	7574.64

NOTE: $e =$ TER = XER = 0.5; ESUBEX = 0.1; ESUBGT = 0.1.

Figure D.4
Optimal values of s for various values of ESUBEX and ESUBGT when G is free to vary and NEED = 1.0. XER = TER = e 0.5. All lines represent an approximate fit of the points obtained in the simulation.

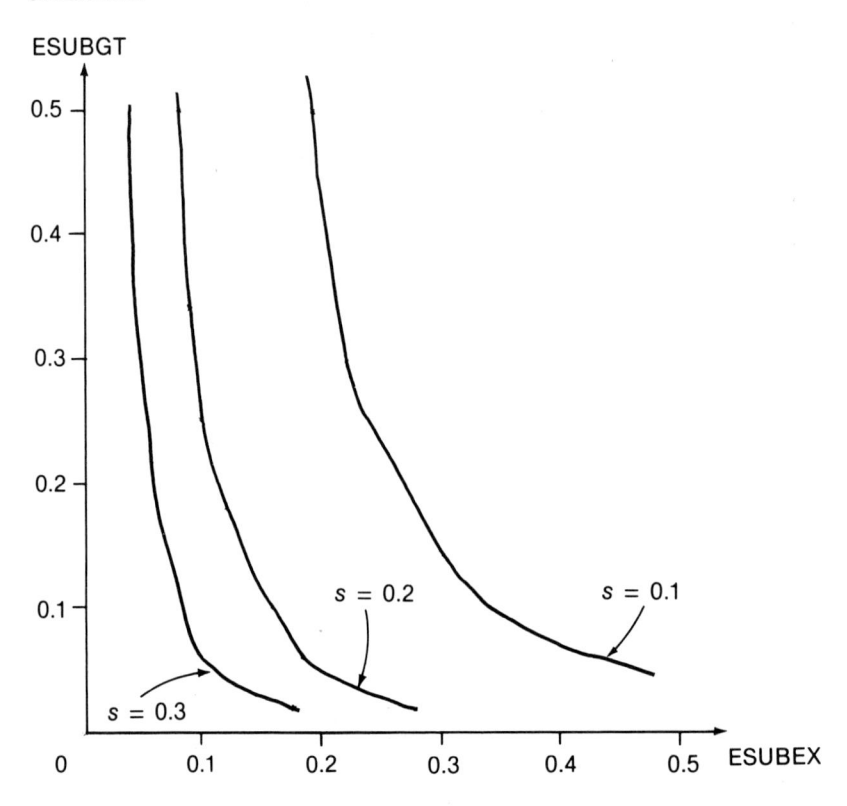

$G = 4000$, $t = 0.5$, and the need commodity is not subsidized ($s = 0$). In the second column, G and t are allowed to vary, holding government revenue constant, and again allowing no subsidy; this produces the negative income tax (G and t) that maximizes social welfare. Finally the third column allows G, t, and s to vary, holding government revenue fixed. This produces the combination of cash transfers (the negative income tax) and in-kind subsidy that maximizes social welfare.

The results in Table D.5 are striking. When the variation in need is low (NEED = 0.5), then income redistribution alone raises SUMU (the social welfare

Simulations of inability and optimal subsidies 145

Figure D.5
Optimal values of s for various values of ESUBEX and ESUBGT when G is free to vary and NEED = 1.4. XER = TER = e = 0.5. All lines represent an approximate fit of the points obtained in the simulation.

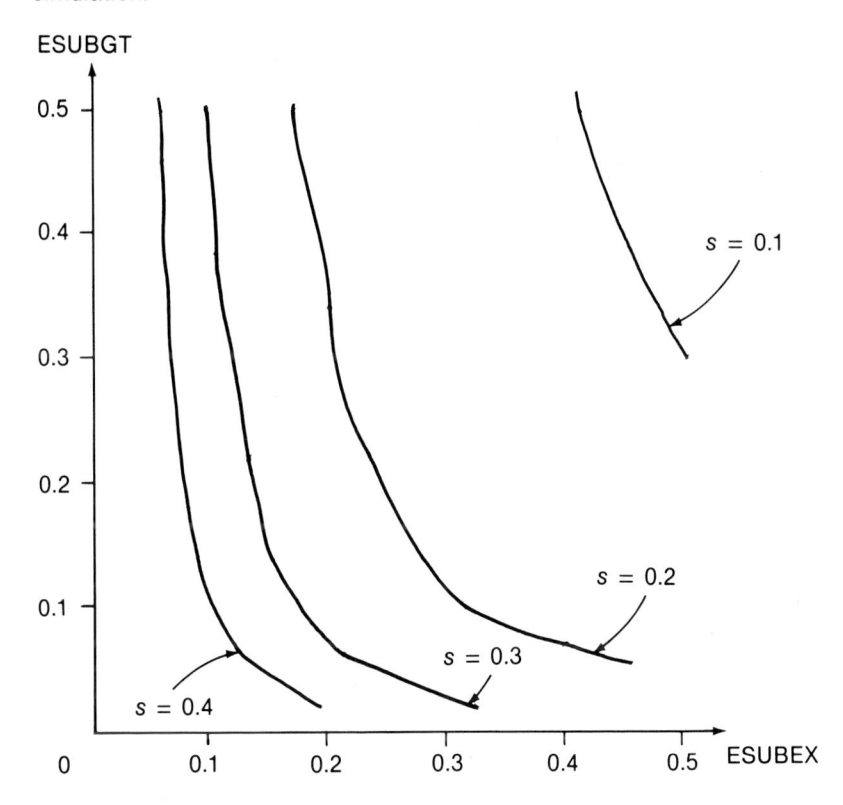

function) almost to its maximum; freeing the subsidy rate s adds little to social welfare. As the variation in need increases, the role of the subsidy rate becomes ever more important. When NEED = 1.0, income redistribution alone increases SUMU by 5 units; introducing a subsidy raises SUMU by an additional 2 units. When NEED = 1.4, income redistribution alone increases SUMU by 5.5 units; introducing a subsidy raises SUMU by an additional 7 units.[1]

---

[1] These figures are for illustration only, since the starting point of G = 4000, t = 0.5 was chosen arbitrarily.

TABLE D.5
Values of utility when G is allowed to vary

Consumer	NEED = 0.5 G = 4000 s = 0 t = 0.5	G = 5563 s = 0 t = 0.612	G = 5500 s = 0.057 t = 0.624	NEED = 1.0 G = 4000 s = 0 t = 0.5	G = 5750 s = 0 t = 0.620	G = 5000 s = 0.275 t = 0.656	NEED = 1.4 G = 4000 s = 0 t = 0.5	G = 5813 s = 0 t = 0.620	G = 4750 s = 0.407 t = 0.686
1 ($W = 2, N = 0$)	66.98	69.89	69.94	66.98	70.36	69.52	66.98	70.58	69.21
2 ($W = 2, N = 2000$)	63.54	66.38	66.56	59.91	63.17	63.76	56.84	60.30	62.10
3 ($W = 2, N = 4000$)	59.91	62.68	63.01	51.88	55.05	57.43	44.43	47.87	54.06
4 ($W = 4, N = 0$)	75.36	76.27	76.26	75.36	76.54	75.90	75.36	76.70	75.48
5 ($W = 4, N = 2000$)	72.96	73.66	73.74	70.49	71.21	71.62	68.45	69.14	70.20
6 ($W = 4, N = 4000$)	70.49	70.96	71.13	65.26	65.44	67.08	60.75	60.64	64.48
7 ($W = 6, N = 0$)	80.58	80.60	80.56	80.58	80.77	80.24	80.58	80.90	79.80
8 ($W = 6, N = 2000$)	78.73	78.51	78.54	76.83	76.50	76.82	75.28	74.86	75.56
9 ($W = 6, N = 4000$)	76.83	76.37	76.47	72.89	71.97	73.24	69.57	68.29	71.07
10 ($W = 8, N = 0$)	84.21	83.77	83.71	84.21	83.87	83.42	84.21	83.98	82.98
11 ($W = 8, N = 2000$)	82.69	82.02	82.02	81.15	80.30	80.56	79.89	78.94	79.43
12 ($W = 8, N = 4000$)	81.15	80.23	80.29	77.96	76.56	77.60	75.32	73.56	75.71
13 ($W = 12, N = 0$)	88.97	88.13	88.06	88.97	88.16	87.62	88.97	88.25	87.40
14 ($W = 12, N = 2000$)	87.85	86.81	86.78	86.72	85.46	85.65	85.80	84.44	84.70
15 ($W = 12, N = 4000$)	86.72	85.46	85.47	84.41	82.67	83.43	82.51	80.45	81.92
SUMU	7937.54	7942	7942*	7817.06	7822	7824*	7715.54	7721	7728*

NOTE: See note to Table D.4. Asterisk denotes that program was not exact enough to provide more than four-figure accuracy.

IN-KIND TRANSFERS IN MAXIMIZING SOCIAL WELFARE

In general, the results of the two simulations conform with the general predictions of the model. The larger the impact of inability on utility (the larger the highest value of n_i), the larger is the optimal subsidy rate s and the more important is that subsidy in maximizing social welfare. The smaller are the elasticities of substitution, the larger is the optimal value of s.

Notice, however, that the simulations show optimal subsidies of significant size only for very great inability and very small elasticities of substitution. This occurs because both simulations assume a need good X that is consumed by all individuals (although those with inability do tend to consume somewhat more of it). In other words, overuse is a problem affecting all consumers. In reality, many goods whose consumption is associated with inability are useful only to those with a significant amount of inability (wheelchairs are only useful to those who cannot walk, nursing homes to those who cannot care for themselves, and so on).

Furthermore, in the simulations, consumption rises with income. The income elasticity of demand is close to one for those with no inability, so the largest benefits of in-kind subsidies accrue to the wealthy. This does not happen in reality. Most in-kind programs test income, restrict the quantity of a commodity that can be purchased under the subsidy, or provide subsidies to commodities whose demand is relatively income inelastic. (Where the effect of higher income is to demand better quality and not more quantity, programs may also subsidize inferior goods.)

Even given these 'problems' (some of which are examined by computer simulation in Appendix F), the simulations produce positive values for the subsidy. Thus, they make a strong case for the use of in-kind transfers when inability is significant and difficult to measure.

APPENDIX E

Principles for subsidy systems: suggestions by a federal-provincial working party

In 1974, the Federal-Provincial Working Party on Social Services developed a set of principles for subsidy systems. It is interesting to note how many of these principles relate to the theory of inability, as well as to more traditional models described in this book. Economists and social policy-makers use different language, but their concerns are not always unrelated.

Because the Working Party's interim report (there was no final report) is not widely available, these principles are reproduced here:

PRINCIPLES GOVERNING SELECTION OF A USER CHARGE/SUBSIDY SYSTEM
AS DEVELOPED BY THE WORKING PARTY ON SOCIAL SERVICES

i. Where it is desirable to encourage use of a service, for example because of its preventive impact, the service should be free. However, where for other reasons such as total government cost it is not considered desirable for the service to be free, then the subsidy system which provides the next highest degree of subsidization should be considered.

ii. Where it is necessary to provide a service on a mandatory basis for the protection of society or of the individual or his family, it should be free.

iii. Where a service, or a component of a service, is by its nature designed specifically for a section of the population that suffers from some permanent disadvantage (the disabled, mentally handicapped, etc.), it should be free.

iv. Where society has recognized that it has a collective responsibility to provide a service, whether or not an individual could provide it for himself, then that service should be provided free. This recognition will most likely occur when most members of the general population have recognized that they themselves run the risk of needing that particular service at some time in their lives (e.g. hospital and medical).

v. Where a service replaces another service that is free, it should be free.

vi. Where a service is seen as necessary for the general public good, and could not be economically self supporting if it were totally unsubsidized, then a partial universal subsidy might be considered.

vii. Where a service, or an element of a service, is normally required by everyone, and financed out of one's own income, it should not be free; a user charge should be levied up to the normal cost of the service. (e.g. transportation). However, where special needs create costs above normal or ordinary costs the increased costs should be fully subsidized; that is, the service should be benchmarked. This of course assumes that income security payments will be high enough to cover the normal costs of living.

viii. Where a service is normally required by everyone and income security payments are high enough to take account of the costs of the service (e.g. food and clothing), the service should be unsubsidized.

ix. Where society has recognized that it has a collective responsibility to ensure that everyone who needs a service can afford to purchase it, then a charge may be made for the service based on the recipients' ability to pay. Such a charge may be justified to reduce the overall charge to society and to reduce any apparent inequity between users and non-users. This, of course, implies that if the recipient is unable to afford anything towards the cost of the service, then there will be no user charge in that case. (Working Party on Social Services 1974, 85-6)

Principles iii, iv, v, vii, and viii coincide with the theory of inability developed in Chapter 3. Principle iii refers to inability that occurs at birth; it cannot, therefore, be privately insured and hence requires social insurance. Principle iv refers to inability that might be privately insured but that society, for various reasons, judges to require public insurance programs. Principle v deals with close substitutes, an issue discussed in Chapter 4. Principle vii suggests that, where possible, subsidies should be given to goods used only by persons with inability and that these subsidies should be an attempt to compensate for the degree of inability present; this idea is also discussed in Chapter 4. Finally, principle viii suggests an important part of the theory of inability: that inability is only an issue when it varies significantly among individuals. When all families of a given income consume similar amounts of a commodity, or when inability can be measured easily (say be family size), no in-kind subsidy is appropriate.

The remaining principles are less clearly connected to inability. Principle i concerns the desirability of subsidizing preventive services. If these services prevent inability, then it is logical to encourage the prevention of conditions that may later call for much larger expenditures. (Private insurance also invests in preventive activity.) If these services address the young, motives of paternalism may also be present. Principle ii suggests giving full subsidies to protective services for reasons of conventional externalities (protecting society) and paternalism (protecting the individual). Principle vi concerns the general public good and seems to address the issue of conventional externalities in both production and consumption. Finally, principle ix deals with the issue of income-testing when inability varies (see Chapter 4).

APPENDIX F

Computer simulations targeting a subsidy for inability and/or low income

The computer simulations described in Appendix D were rerun for a large number of cases, first targeting the subsidy by limiting it to consumers with significant inability, then to consumers to low incomes (with and without targeting for inability. All variables were defined as in Appendix D.

TARGETING ACCORDING TO INABILITY

The first computer simulation in this run limited the subsidy to the groups with above-average inability. Table F.1 compares the results, for a number of selected cases. In each case, government revenue is held constant and the simulation run with no subsidy, with an equal subsidy for all consumers, with a subsidy for all consumers with inability (all-consumers for whom N_i = 2000 or 4000), and with a subsidy only for consumers with the greatest inability (all consumers for whom N_i = 4000). In all cases, the two simulations of targeting increase social welfare, although whether it is best to aim at all inability or only at extreme inability varies from case to case.

Tables F.2 and F.3 examine one case in detail. All the subsidies redistribute from those with no inability to those with inability (relative to the run in which there is no subsidy, but G and t are varied to maximize social welfare subject to the equal revenue constraint). As we saw in Appendix D, a subsidy that goes to all consumers preserves the order of well-being within each income class (so that those with more inability have lower utilities). The targeted subsidies do not preserve this order, a phenomenon often criticized in real programs. For example, the subsidy to all consumers with inability (N_i = 2000 or 4000) frequently makes some who have moderate inability (N_i = 2000) better off than others who have the same incomes but no inability. (In both Tables F.2 and F.3, compare consumers 4 and 5, 7 and 8, 10 and 11, and 13 and 14.) The subsidy to

TABLE F.1
Subsidizing only persons with inability: the effects on optimal s, optimal G, and SUMU

NEED	ESUBEX	ESUBGT	No subsidy SUMU	Subsidy to all consumers Optimal s	G	Increase in SUMU	Subsidy to consumers with inability Optimal s	G	Increase in SUMU	Subsidy to extremely inable Optimal s	G	Increase in SUMU
1.0	0.05	0.05	8093	0.457	6500	5	0.453	7250	10	0.449	7625	9
1.0	0.05	0.10	7915	0.435	4500	3	0.437	5188	7	0.443	5438	6
1.0	0.05	0.50	7205	0.271	875	1	0.307	875	2	0.341	875	2
1.0	0.10	0.05	7998	0.321	6938	3	0.421	7250	9	0.425	7625	8
1.0	0.10	0.10	7822	0.275	5000	2	0.387	5250	7	0.414	5375	6
1.0	0.10	0.50	7149	0.165	1000	1	0.263	938	2	0.301	1000	2
1.0	0.50	0.05	7467	0.093	7688	1	0.261	7625	6	0.308	7750	6
1.0	0.50	0.10	7306	0.072	5563	0	0.223	5500	3	0.275	5500	3
1.0	0.50	0.50	6841	0.040	1156	0	0.135	1063	1	0.182	1063	1
1.4	0.10	0.10	7721	0.407	4750	7	0.489	5125	15	0.496	5375	13
1.4	0.10	0.20	7426	0.357	2750	4	0.450	2938	10	0.468	3188	9
1.4	0.10	0.30	7234	0.328	1750	3	0.420	1813	8	0.441	2000	7
1.4	0.20	0.10	7536	0.283	5000	4	0.422	5250	12	0.442	5563	11
1.4	0.20	0.20	7261	0.232	3000	3	0.377	3063	8	0.412	3250	8
1.4	0.20	0.30	7092	0.205	2000	2	0.348	1938	7	0.387	2063	7
1.4	0.30	0.10	7389	0.208	5250	3	0.379	5250	11	0.409	5563	10
1.4	0.30	0.20	7131	0.167	3188	2	0.330	3125	7	0.374	3250	7
1.4	0.30	0.30	6982	0.149	2125	1	0.302	2000	5	0.352	2000	5

NOTE: e = XER = TER = 0.5. SUMU with no subsidy (s = 0) is calculated with G varying to optimum; subsequent increases in SUMU are based upon this amount.

TABLE F.2
Subsidizing only the inable when NEED = 1.0: the effect on utility

Consumer		Utility with no subsidy ($s = 0, G = 5750$, $t = 0.620$)	Utility with subsidy to all ($s = 0.275, G = 5000$, $t = 0.656$)	Utility with subsidy to all inable ($s = 0.387, G = 5250$, $t = 0.656$)	Utility with subsidy to extremely inable ($s = 0.414, G = 5375$, $t = 0.636$)
1	($W = 2, N = 0$)	70.36	69.52	67.84	68.73
2	($W = 2, N = 2000$)	63.17	63.76	66.81	61.27
3	($W = 2, N = 4000$)	55.05	57.43	61.58	63.48
4	($W = 4, N = 0$)	76.54	75.90	74.19	75.12
5	($W = 4, N = 2000$)	71.21	71.62	74.07	69.59
6	($W = 4, N = 4000$)	65.44	67.08	70.28	72.01
7	($W = 6, N = 0$)	80.77	80.24	78.60	79.50
8	($W = 6, N = 2000$)	76.50	76.82	78.90	75.08
9	($W = 6, N = 4000$)	71.97	73.24	75.90	77.47
10	($W = 8, N = 0$)	83.87	83.42	81.86	82.73
11	($W = 8, N = 2000$)	80.30	80.56	82.38	79.02
12	($W = 8, N = 4000$)	76.56	77.60	79.88	81.33
13	($W = 12, N = 0$)	88.16	87.82	86.41	87.20
14	($W = 12, N = 2000$)	85.46	85.65	87.12	84.40
15	($W = 12, N = 4000$)	82.67	83.43	85.25	86.48
SUMU		7822	7824	7829	7828

NOTE: e = XER = TER = 0.5; ESUBEX = 0.1, ESUBGT = 0.1.

TABLE F.3

Subsidizing only the inable when NEED = 1.4: the effect on utility

Consumer		Utility with no subsidy ($s = 0, G = 5813, t = 0.620$)	Utility with subsidy to all ($s = 0.047, G = 4750, t = 0.686$)	Utility with subsidy to all with inability ($s = 0.489, G = 5125, t = 0.673$)	Utility with subsidy to those with extreme inability ($s = 0.496, G = 5375, t = 0.650$)
1	($W = 2, N = 0$)	70.58	69.21	66.99	68.42
2	($W = 2, N = 2000$)	60.30	62.10	66.01	57.55
3	($W = 2, N = 4000$)	47.87	54.06	59.49	61.72
4	($W = 4, N = 0$)	76.70	75.48	73.32	74.71
5	($W = 4, N = 2000$)	69.14	70.20	73.44	66.69
6	($W = 4, N = 4000$)	60.64	64.48	68.74	70.73
7	($W = 6, N = 0$)	80.90	79.80	77.74	79.07
8	($W = 6, N = 2000$)	74.86	75.56	78.37	72.65
9	($W = 6, N = 4000$)	68.29	71.07	74.66	76.45
10	($W = 8, N = 0$)	83.98	82.98	81.04	82.29
11	($W = 8, N = 2000$)	78.94	79.43	81.92	76.92
12	($W = 8, N = 4000$)	73.56	75.71	78.84	80.74
13	($W = 12, N = 0$)	88.25	87.40	85.67	86.78
14	($W = 12, N = 2000$)	84.44	84.70	86.76	82.71
15	($W = 12, N = 4000$)	80.45	81.92	84.45	85.83
SUMU		7721	7728	7736	7734

NOTE: e = XER = TER = 0.5; ESUBEX = 0.1, ESUBGT = 0.1.

Targeting for inability and/or low income 155

only those consumers with great inability (N_i = 4000) often makes them better off than those who have the same incomes but less inability (N_i = 2000). (Compare consumers 2 and 3, 5 and 6, 8 and 9, 11 and 12, and 14 and 15.)

TARGETING ACCORDING TO INCOME

Next the computer simulation was rerun to examine the results of an approximation of income-testing.

Again G and t were also allowed to vary, holding government revenue constant. Initially, no subsidy is given, the optimal values of G and t are determined, and SUMU (the additive social welfare function) is computed. Then different subsidies, all limited by wage rate, are introduced. The first goes to all low-income consumers ($W < 6$ or consumers 1 through 9 in Tables F.2 and F.3); the next to all low-income consumers who have a significant amount of inability (N_i = 2000 or 4000 – consumers 2, 3, 5, 6, 8, and 9 in the earlier tables); the last to only those consumers who have both low incomes and great inability (N_i = 4000).

The results are reported in Table F.4. When they are compared with those in Table F.3, it is clear that income-testing raises the optimal subsidy significantly. This is not surprising, since the subsidy now contains a significant amount of income redistribution, quite independent of inability. Several other, less expected results also emerge. First, an increase in NEED (indicating an increase in the variation of inability within the population) always increases the optimal value of the subsidy and may make quite a large one justifiable. Second, limiting an income-tested subsidy to persons with inability does not clearly raise the optimal subsidy because of the income redistribution that occurs as a result of the income test. This result may be particularly striking here because of the peculiar way that the subsidy was set in the model. Although income tests usually relate the subsidy rate to earned income, this model uses a subsidy rate that falls with the wage rate. Thus, those receiving the subsidy do not face the usual work disincentive.[1]

This is not to suggest that income tests cannot be useful. The large increases in SUMU with the income test (much larger than the increases in SUMU when the subsidy is not income-tested) attest to the desirability of targeting the subsidy to the poor. Moreover, Tables F.2 and F.3 show that all the subsidies that do not use an income test end up benefiting consumer 15 (high inability and high

---

1 The model was set up this way because computational difficulties precluded further complications in the income test.

TABLE F.4

Income-testing: the effects on optimal s, optimal G, and SUMU when the subsidy goes only to persons for whom $W_i \leq 6$

NEED	ESUBEX	ESUBGT	No subsidy SUMU	Subsidy to all with low incomes Optimal s	G	Increase in SUMU	Subsidy to all inable with low incomes Optimal s	G	Increase in SUMU	Subsidy to extremely inable with low incomes Optimal s	G	Increase in SUMU
1.0	0.05	0.05	8093	0.908	6563	125	0.899	7250	72	0.888	7625	42
1.0	0.05	0.10	7915	0.908	4938	108	0.903	5313	61	0.896	5531	36
1.0	0.05	0.50	7205	0.870	688	69	0.864	625	39	0.855	875	23
1.0	0.10	0.05	7998	0.839	6688	109	0.837	7250	65	0.826	7625	39
1.0	0.10	0.10	7822	0.839	5000	94	0.836	5375	55	0.830	5563	33
1.0	0.10	0.50	7149	0.782	750	58	0.781	750	34	0.776	1000	20
1.0	0.50	0.05	7467	0.571	7250	61	0.603	7625	42	0.610	7813	27
1.0	0.50	0.10	7306	0.562	5375	50	0.593	5500	34	0.600	5688	22
1.0	0.50	0.50	6841	0.479	938	30	0.516	938	20	0.530	1000	13
1.4	0.10	0.10	7721	0.847	4969	111	0.853	5375	76	0.844	5625	47
1.4	0.10	0.20	7426	0.837	3000	92	0.846	3125	61	0.839	3313	39
1.4	0.10	0.30	7234	0.824	1875	81	0.833	2000	54	0.830	2000	34
1.4	0.20	0.10	7536	0.750	5125	91	0.768	5500	64	0.766	5688	41
1.4	0.20	0.20	7261	0.734	3125	74	0.757	3125	52	0.755	3375	34
1.4	0.20	0.30	7092	0.718	1875	66	0.741	2000	47	0.742	2125	30
1.4	0.30	0.10	7389	0.683	5125	78	0.709	5563	58	0.712	5625	38
1.4	0.30	0.20	7131	0.661	3188	64	0.696	3000	47	0.696	3500	31
1.4	0.30	0.30	6982	0.643	2000	55	0.677	2063	41	0.683	2188	27

NOTE: See note to Table F.1.

income), a consumer in the top part of the income distribution who has relatively high utility (and hence lower marginal utility of income). The same subsidies harm some low-income consumers (consumers 1 and 4, for example). This inequity obviously cuts the desirability of the programs and suggests the superiority of income-testing in many circumstances.

Bibliography

Aaron, H.J. (1975) 'Alternative ways to increase work effort under income maintenance systems.' Chapter 6 of Lurie (1975)
Aaron, H.J. and G.M. von Furstenberg (1971) 'The inefficiency of transfers in kind: the case of housing assistance.' *Western Economic Journal* 9, 184-91
Akerlof, G.A. (1970) 'The market for lemons: qualitative uncertainty and the market mechanism.' *Quarterly Journal of Economics* 84, 488-500
− (1978) 'The economics of "tagging" as applied to the optimal income tax, welfare programs, and manpower planning.' *American Economic Review* 68, 8-19
Arrow, K.J. (1971) 'A utilitarian approach to the concept of equality in public expenditures.' *Quarterly Journal of Economics* 85, 409-15
Barmack, J.A. (1977) 'The case against in-kind transfers: the food stamp program.' *Policy Analysis* 3, 509-30
Barer, M.L., R.G. Evans, and G.L. Stoddart (1979) *Controlling Health Care Costs by Direct Charges to Patients: Snare or Delusion?* Ontario Economic Council Occasional Paper 10 (Toronto)
Baumol, W.J. and D.F. Bradford (1970) 'Optimal departures from marginal cost pricing.' *American Economic Review* 60, 265-83
Bird, R. (1976) *Charging for Public Services: A New Look at an Old Idea.* Canadian Tax Foundation Paper 59 (Toronto)
Brown, J.C. (1977) *A Hit-and-Miss Affair: Policies for Disabled People in Canada* (Ottawa: The Canadian Council on Social Development)
Buchanan, J.M. (1968) 'What kind of redistribution do we want?' *Economica* 40, 185-90
Clarkson, K.W. (1976) 'Welfare benefits of the food stamp program.' *Southern Economic Journal* 43, 864-78

Daly, G. and F. Giertz (1972) 'Welfare Economics and Welfare Reform.' *American Economic Review* 62, 131-8

Derthick, M. (1975) *Uncontrollable Spending for Social Services Grants* (Washington: The Brookings Institution)

Diamond, P.A. and J.A. Mirrlees (1971) 'Optimal taxation and public production.' *American Economic Review* 61: 8-27, 261-78

Dineen, J. (1979) 'CAS in a tug-of-war with tragedy.' *The Toronto Star* 17 February

Feldstein, M.S. (1972) 'Distributional equity and the optimal structure of public prices' *American Economic Review* 62, 32-6

Friedman, M. (1953) *Essays in Positive Economics* (Chicago: University of Chicago Press)

– (1962) *Capitalism and Freedom* (Chicago: The University of Chicago Press)

Galatin, M. (1973) 'A comparison of the benefits of the food-stamp program, free food stamps, and an equivalent cash payment', *Public Policy* 21, 291-302

Garfinkel, I. (1973) 'Is in-kind redistribution efficient?' *Quarterly Journal of Economics* 87, 320-30

Giertz, J.F. and D.H. Sullivan (1977) 'Donor optimization and the food stamp program.' *Public Choice* 29, 19-35

Goode, R. (1964) *The Individual Income Tax* (Washington: The Brookings Institution)

Grubel, H.G., D. Maki, and S. Sax (1975) 'Real and insurance-induced unemployment in Canada.' *Canadian Journal of Economics* 8, 174-91

Hepworth, H.P. (1975) *Residential and Community Services for Old People*. Personal Social Services in Canada: A Review 6 (Ottawa: The Canadian Council on Social Development)

– (1977) *Personal Social Services for the Handicapped*. Personal Social Services in Canada: A Review 2 (Ottawa: The Canadian Council on Social Development)

Hochman, H.M. and J.D. Rodgers (1969) 'Pareto optimal redistribution.' *American Economic Review* 59, 542-57

Hu, T. and N. Knaub (1976) 'Effects of cash and in-kind welfare payments on family expenditures.' *Policy Analysis* 2: 71-92

Kaliski, S.F. (1975) 'Real and insurance-induced unemployment in Canada.' *Canadian Journal of Economics* 8, 600-03

Krashinsky, M. (1977) *Day Care and Public Policy in Ontario*. Ontario Economic Council Research Study 11 (Toronto: University of Toronto Press)

Lalonde, M. (1973) *Working Paper on Social Security in Canada* 2nd ed. (Canada, Ministry of National Health and Welfare, 18 April)

Lancaster, K.J. (1966) 'A new approach to consumer theory.' *Journal of Political Economy* 74, 132-57

LeGrand, J. (1975) 'Public price discrimination and aid to low income groups.' *Economica* 21, 32-42

Lurie, I., ed. (1975) *Integrating Income Maintenance Programs.* (New York: Academic Press)

Mirer, T.W. (1975) 'Alternative approaches to integrating income transfer programs.' Chapter 5 of Lurie (1975)

Mishan, E.J. (1972) 'The futility of pareto-efficient distributions.' *American Economic Review* 62, 971-6

Munk, K.J. (1977) 'Optimal public sector pricing taking the distributional aspect into consideration.' *Quarterly Journal of Economics* 91, 639-50

Musgrave, R.A. (1959) *The Theory of Public Finance* (New York: McGraw-Hill Book Company)

– (1968) 'The role of social insurance in an overall program for social welfare.' In W.G. Bowen et al., *The Princeton Symposium on the American System of Social Insurance* (New York: McGraw-Hill Book Company)

– (1970) 'Pareto optimal redistribution: comment.' *American Economic Review* 60, 991-3

Nicholson, W. (1975) *Intermediate Microeconomics and Its Application* (Winsdale, Ill.: The Dryden Press)

Okun, A.M. (1975) *Equality and Efficiency: The Big Tradeoff* (Washington: The Brookings Institution)

Ontario Economic Council (1976) *Issues and Alternatives, 1976, Social Security.* (Toronto) Pamphlet

– (1979) *Issues and Alternatives: Update 1979* (Toronto)

Ontario, Government of (1978) *The Family Law Reform Act, 1978* (Toronto: Queen's Printer) pamphlet

Ontario Ministry of Community and Social Services (1975) *Do You Need a Visiting Nurse or Homemaker?* Pamphlet

Ontario Ministry of Community and Social Services, Senior Citizen's Branch (1978a) 'Alternatives to constitutional care for senior citizens projects.' Memo 16/78

– (1978b) 'Financial statistics for the 12-month period ending December 31, 1977.' Photocopy

Pauly, M.V. (1970) 'Efficiency in the provision of consumption subsidies.' *Kyklos* 23, 33-57

Peltzman, S. (1975) 'The effects of automobile safety regulation.' *Journal of Political Economy* 83, 677-725

Posner, R.A. (1977) *Economic Analysis of Law* 2nd ed. (Boston: Little, Brown and Company)

Rawls, J. (1971) *A Theory of Justice* (Cambridge, Mass.: Harvard University Press, The Belknap Press)

Revenue Canada (1978) *Your Tax Guide.* Pamphlet accompanying federal income tax forms

Rothschild, M. and J. Stiglitz (1976) 'Equilibrium in competitive insurance markets: an essay on the economics of imperfect information.' *Quarterly Journal of Economics* 90, 629-49

Samuelson, P.A. (1955) 'The pure theory of public expenditure.' *Review of Economics and Statistics* 37, 350-56

Schmundt, M., E. Smolensky, and L. Stiefel, (1975) 'When do recipients value transfers at their costs to taxpayers?' Chap. 7 of Lurie (1975)

Simon, J.G. (1978) 'Charity and Dynasty under the Federal Tax System.' *The Probate Lawyer* 5, 1-92

Smeeding, T.M. (1977) 'The anti-poverty effectiveness of in-kind transfers.' *The Journal of Human Resources* 12, 360-78

Stigler, G.J. and G.S. Becker (1977) 'De gustibus non est disputandum.' *American Economic Review* 67, 76-90

Streeten, P. and S.J. Burki (1978) 'Basic Needs: Some Issues.' *World Development* 6, 411-21

Tesher, E. (1979) 'Eleven Years in Chronic Care.' *The Toronto Star* 23 January

Thurow, L.C. (1974) 'Cash versus in kind transfers.' *American Economic Review* 64, 190-95.

Tobin, J. (1970) 'On limiting the domain of inequality.' *Journal of Law and Economics* 13, 263-77

U.S. Department of Health, Education, and Welfare, Office of Child Development (1967) *Standards and Costs for Day Care.* Unpublished, photocopy

Weitzman, M.L. (1977) 'Is the price system or rationing more effective in getting a commodity to those who need it most?' *The Bell Journal of Economics* 8, 517-24

Working Party on Social Services (1974) 'Federal-provincial social security review, Interim Report on Social Services in Canada.' Report of the Working Party on Social Services to the Continuing Committee on Social Security, Document no. 120. Photocopy

Yandle, B. (1974) 'Welfare programs and donor-recipient adjustments.' *Public Finance Quarterly* 2, 322-9

Zeckhauser, R.J. (1971) 'Optimal mechanisms for income transfer.' *American Economic Review* 61, 324-34

Zeckhauser, R.J. and P. Schuck (1970) 'An alternative to the Nixon income maintenance plan: a solution to the problem of work incentives.' *Public Interest* no. 19, 120-30